RelAndXML
A System to Manage
XML-based Course Material with
Object-Relational Databases

Dissertation
zur Erlangung des Grades
»Doktor der Naturwissenschaften«

am Fachbereich Mathematik und Informatik
der Johannes Gutenberg-Universität in Mainz

vorgelegt von

Astrid Susanne Schnädelbach

geboren in Kaiserslautern

Mainz, im August 2003

Bibliografische Information Der Deutschen Bibliothek

Die Deutsche Bibliothek verzeichnet diese Publikation in der Deutschen
Nationalbibliografie; detaillierte bibliografische Daten sind im Internet über
http://dnb.ddb.de abrufbar.

ISBN 3-8325-0517-2

Logos Verlag Berlin
Comeniushof, Gubener Str. 47,
10243 Berlin
Tel.: +49 030 42 85 10 90
Fax: +49 030 42 85 10 92
INTERNET: http://www.logos-verlag.de

Berichterstatter: Universitätsprofessor Dr. Herbert Göttler
                     Privatdozent Dr. Klaus Barthelmann

Tag der mündlichen Prüfung: 10. Februar 2004

D 77 (Dissertation an der Johannes Gutenberg-Universität Mainz)

Zusammenfassung

Die vorliegende Arbeit beschreibt das im Rahmen dieses Dissertationsprojekts implementierte System *RelAndXML*, das für das Management und die Speicherung von hypertextzentrierten XML-Dokumenten und den dazugehörenden XSL-Stylesheet-Dokumenten spezialisiert ist.

Der Anwendungsbereich sind die Vorlesungsmaterialien an der Universität. Typischerweise werden einige Übungsaufgaben in den Folgejahren wiederverwendet, andere aber auch durch neue Aufgaben ersetzt. Zur Zeit verwenden die wissenschaftlichen Mitarbeiterinnen und Mitarbeiter unterschiedliche Textverarbeitungssysteme, außerdem ist nicht immer sichergestellt, dass die Dateien mit den Aufgaben aus vergangenen Jahren auch zur Verfügung stehen. Daher werden manchmal die gleichen Aufgaben erneut eingetippt. *RelAndXML* löst dieses Problem dadurch, dass die in XML geschriebenen Übungsblätter, aufgeteilt in *Textbausteine* sowie sonstige Teile, in einer speziellen Datenbank abgelegt werden. *RelAndXML* kann aber auch für andere Anwendungsbereiche verwendet werden, indem einfach das Kernschema der Datenbank durch ein anderes, zum Beispiel für technische Dokumentationen, ersetzt wird.

Die Speicherung von XML-Dokumenten in Datenbanken ist seit einigen Jahren ein wichtiges Thema der Datenbankforschung. Ansätze dafür sind von dem jeweiligen Anwendungsbereich abhängig und gliedern sich in solche für datenzentrierte und andere für dokumentenzentrierte Dokumente. *Datenzentrierte* XML-Dokumente sind gültig in Bezug auf eine Document Type Definition (DTD), sie haben wenig gemischten Inhalt und die Reihenfolge innerhalb des Dokuments ist weitgehend unwichtig. Um datenzentrierte Dokumente in einer (objekt-) relationalen Datenbank zu speichern, definiert man eine Abbildung zwischen der DTD und dem Datenbankschema. Da unser Hypertext keiner DTD genügt, können wir keinen der bekannten datenzentrierten Ansätze verwenden. *Dokumentenzentriertes* XML hat keine DTD, ist also nicht gültig, stattdessen gibt es einen relativ hohen Anteil an gemischtem Inhalt und die Reihenfolge innerhalb des Dokuments ist sehr wichtig. Die bisher bekannten Ansätze zur Speicherung von dokumentenzentriertem XML erlauben leider nicht die Wiederverwendung von Textbausteinen.

Die vorliegende Arbeit präsentiert einen Ansatz zur Speicherung von hypertextzentrierten XML-Dokumenten, der Aspekte von datenzentrierten und dokumentenzentrierten Ansätzen kombiniert. Der Ansatz erlaubt die Wiederverwendung von Textbausteinen und speichert die Reihenfolge dort, wo sie wichtig ist. Mit *RelAndXML* können nicht nur Elemente gespeichert werden, wie mit einigen anderen Ansätzen, sondern auch Attribute, Kommentare und Processing Instructions.

RelAndXML wurde mit Java und unter Verwendung einer objekt-relationalen Datenbank implementiert. Das System hat eine graphische Benutzungsoberfläche, die das Erstellen und Verändern der XML- und XSL-Dokumente, das Einfügen von neuen oder schon gespeicherten Textbausteinen sowie das Erzeugen von HTML-Dokumenten zur Veröffentlichung ermöglicht.

Abstract

In this thesis, we present our newly invented system *RelAndXML* for the management and storage of hypertext-centric XML documents and the according XSL stylesheets.

Our sample application area is the course material at university. Typically, course material is being reused on multiple assignments, while it is also important to add or replace questions. Currently, teaching assistants use different word processors and the availability of previous year's assignment files is not always certain. This results sometimes in retyping the same questions. *RelAndXML* offers a solution to this problem by saving the XML formatted assignments as text modules and other parts in a special database. However, *RelAndXML* is not restricted to this application area, since the core schema can easily be replaced, e.g. by a schema for technical online manuals.

Storing XML documents in databases has been a major topic in database research in the last few years. Approaches on this topic are dependent on the desired application area and can be divided into two main directions: some concentrate on data-centric and others on document-centric documents. *Data-centric* XML documents are valid with respect to a document type definition (DTD), they have sparse mixed content and the order in which subelements and PCDATA occur is usually unimportant. The concept for storing data-centric XML in (object-) relational database systems is to define a mapping between the DTD and the database schema. Since our hypertext does not conform to a DTD, we cannot use a data-centric approach on its own. *Document-centric* XML often has no DTD such that it is non-valid XML, mixed content often occurs, and the document order does matter. The known document-centric approaches do preserve document order, but they make reusing text modules impossible.

In this thesis, we present a hypertext-centric approach that combines aspects of data-centric as well as document-centric approaches. It enables the reuse of text modules and preserves document order where necessary. Another important feature of *RelAndXML* is that it supports not only XML elements, but also attributes, comments, and processing instructions.

RelAndXML is a Java-implemented system using an object-relational database. It provides a graphical user interface which allows to create and update the XML and XSL parts of hypertext documents, to insert new or saved text modules, and to generate HTML or XHTML output documents.

Acknowledgements

I would like to thank my supervisor Prof. Dr. Herbert Göttler for the possibility to write this thesis and for the valuable discussions concerning the research presented.

I thank PD Dr. Klaus Barthelmann for his helpful advice and sound support during the whole time and especially in the later stages of this project.

Thanks to Prof. Dr. Thomas Schwentick for the constructive discussions during the early stages of this project.

Many thanks to my friends Dr. Nina Balz, Dr. Susanne Kruse, Dr. Nicole Schweikardt, and to my brother Holger Schnädelbach, for sharing the PhD time with me and for careful proofreading.

Special thanks to everybody who helped and encouraged me during the past years.

Finally, I would like to thank my family for their support.

Contents

Chapter 1

Introduction

1.1 Motivation

The aim of this research project is to design and implement a system for the management and storage of academic course material such as assignments and examinations.

Typically, the teaching assistant responsible for the questions on the assignments of a specific course changes every other year. Different teaching assistants use different word processors like Microsoft Word or LaTeX, or write their assignments in HTML.

However, it is a common and useful practice to reuse questions from the previous years, especially those with a high learning impact. Of course, new questions are also added, in particular for examinations. But the availability and compatibility of previous years' document files is not always certain. This results sometimes in retyping the same questions. There also is no tool for the search of questions about a specific topic.

In this thesis, we present a solution to these problems: we use XML as unified data format and store all the assignments with their questions in such a way that old assignments can be reproduced any time and that new assignments can be assembled from reused as well as new questions.

Let us take a short look at the structure of assignments. They usually consist of a header with the course name, date, number, etc., and several questions, possibly having several parts. We also find various hints, notes about the exam, and holiday greetings. To summarise, these documents have a number of regularly occurring text modules (course, question, part) and a number of irregular and seldomly occurring parts (hints, notes, greetings); we call this *hypertext-centric*. We design our system not just for academic course material, but more generally for hypertext-centric documents.

Storing XML documents in databases has been a major topic in database research in the last few years [CFP00, Wid99]. Approaches on this topic depend on the desired application area and can be divided into two main directions: some concentrate on data-centric and others on document-centric documents [Bou03a].

Data-centric documents are usually valid XML documents (i.e., they have a fairly regular structure which can be described by a DTD) with sparse mixed content, and the order in which subelements and PCDATA occur is usually irrelevant. *Document-centric* XML is often non-valid XML (meaning having no DTD), mixed content occurs often and order does matter. The distinction between data-centric and document-centric can be subtle, and some documents could be viewed either way. In a hypertext application area, documents are written as a combination of new and existing text modules. Most of the text modules are data-centric, but their occurrence within the document is not very restricted and also, free text might be allowed in between text modules. The document order is very important, e.g. a book is not just a *set* of chapters, but the *ordering* of the chapters is very important.

The concept for storing data-centric XML in (object-) relational database systems is to define a mapping between the DTD and the database schema [Bou03c, KKR01, RP02, STH+99]. The advantages of these mappings are that query writing is easy and that the DBMS (or the XML Parser using the DTD) checks data consistency.

Known storage concepts for document-centric XML are different. They either store the entire document without fragmenting and concentrate on fast search algorithms (full-text and indexing) [Tam03]. Other approaches for storing arbitrary XML documents fragment down to every single element [FK99b, Kud01, SYU99] – giving a large number of database tuples per document. This makes queries on the documents and their reconstruction expensive.

For these reasons, we were looking for a suitable approach for a hypertext application area, where documents are written as a combination of new and existing text modules. In such documents, the document order is important. All the quoted document-centric approaches do preserve document order, but they make reusing text modules impossible. The data-centric approaches are not suitable either, since our hypertext does not conform to a DTD.

In this thesis we present our new concept for storing hypertext-centric XML and call it *RelAndXML*. It is a combination of a data-centric with a document-centric approach, saving the structured part in a *Core* schema and the remaining data in an *Extension* schema. This approach allows us to store document-structured data and still keep the mentioned advantages for the structured part of the data. We support not just XML elements (like [FK99b] does), but also attributes, comments, and processing instructions. We concentrate on text sizes usually found on local computers, RelAndXML is not designed for mass data. It preserves document order and allows storing and updating text modules. Additional features include searching assignment questions by keywords and exporting in HTML via XSL.

1.2 Scope

General Features

RelAndXML is a system that manages a collection of hypertext documents. These documents consist of some regular text modules but might also contain some additional text modules whose structure and number is not restricted. Each hypertext document is stored in two parts: an XML document encloses the content and structure of the document whereas an XSL document contains the corresponding stylesheet. The document order of the original document – the order in which text modules, figures, etc. appear in the document – must be preserved, but document order information might be spread on the XML document and on the stylesheet.

RelAndXML provides a graphical user interface (GUI) which allows the creation and update of the XML and XSL parts of hypertext documents, the insertion of new or saved text modules and the production of HTML or XHTML as output document. Since *Rel-AndXML* is not a web server, the documents must be transferred to a web server to be published. Therefore, the system enables users to save both the XML and the XSLT part of documents or the (X)HTML output document to files. We note that only newer browsers like Internet Explorer 5.5 and later or Netscape 6.0 and later display XML documents with a corresponding XSL stylesheet or XHTML documents correctly. Therefore, it is preferable to publish HTML documents as long as older web browsers like Netscape 4.7 are used widely.

RelAndXML is not restricted to a specific application area. Given some meta data about the desired application area, the system is able to save a matching document collection.

RelAndXML is a Java-implemented system using an object-relational database (PostgreSQL or IBM DB2). XML documents are fragmented into parts of useful size. Efficient algorithms for composing and decomposing are provided. "Efficient" here refers to a minimization of the number of database accesses, since on a client/server environment, they are the main time consumers.

Course Material

We have chosen the academic course material as application area for this thesis, especially assignments and examinations. These documents contain some questions, each possibly including several parts or figures. In addition, they usually enclose information about the course, the lecturer, and the teaching assistant. Examinations include rules that must be followed during the exam and a section for summarizing the marking. All these regular document parts are the above-mentioned text modules. Apart from this information that is usually included, *RelAndXML* provides ways to save additional information: An example are the keywords which can be assigned to text modules to simplify the search on a specific topic. A second example is that a question, which is a sequel of another one, can be linked to this other question. The XML document contains this additional information, which can be used within the system, but need not be published. The user can write two different stylesheets – one for the document to be handed out to students, and one with additional internal information.

Identifiers, Versioning, and Publishing

RelAndXML uses identifiers, version numbers, and an attribute called published for the text modules, also called *objects*, in a document. These aspects are explained in the following using short examples with course material.

The user must provide an object identifier, called *user (generated) identifier* (uid) for each object. If the uids are chosen thoughtfully, they make finding objects very easy.

Example 1:   The first assignment of the course "Databases 1" in the summer semester 2002 gets the uid "DB1_Su2002_A1".

It is also possible to save versions of objects. This means they have the same uid, but different version numbers.

Example 2:   In summer 2001, assignment 1 included a question with uid "DB1_Su2001_A1_Q1", so this is version "1.0" of the question. The assignment 1 in summer 2002 includes a slightly different version of this question, thus the uid remains unchanged and the version number is "2.0".

RelAndXML is also an archive for documents. Objects that have been published should not be changed. Therefore, each object has a boolean attribute published.

Example 2 (continued): Since the question with uid "DB1_Su2001_A1_Q1" and version number "1.0" was published in summer 2001, the system forces the user to change the version number, in order to be allowed to make any changes. Experience in programming shows that this is safer than relying on the user's responsibility.

Example 3: The assignment 2 with uid "DB1_Su2002_A2" and version "1.0" was published on June 24. The author wants to correct a mistake in one question on June 27. Since the object has been published, the author must increase the version number in order to change the document. This way, the difference between the version handed out to students and the one published on the web server is documented in the system.

The system uses additional *system (generated) identifiers* (sid) for XML objects, which cannot be changed by the user and which are unique within the database.

Reconstruction and Standard Queries

The most important query is the *reconstruction* of documents or parts of it. Apart from this, the system should (at least) be able to answer queries of the following kind:

- Find all questions with paragraphs containing the term "ER schema".

- Has this question been used on an examination before?

- Find all assignments with questions about "Finite Automata". (Keywords must have been assigned by the authors of the assignments.)

1.3 Organization of this Thesis

The remainder of this thesis is organised as follows:

In Chapter 2, we give an insight into the data format and structure of hypertext-centric XML documents as well as data-centric XSL documents which we want to store in *RelAndXML*. We also introduce some running examples that will be used in later chapters.

In Chapter 3, we check several database types for their ability to store hypertext-centric XML efficiently. We give reasons why we use an object-relational database management system (ORDBMS) for *RelAndXML*. Then, we describe various features of ORDBMS products that we considered using for our system.

Chapter 4 describes approaches for the storage of data-centric as well as document-centric approaches and gathers information on aspects that are important for the storage of hypertext-centric XML.

In Chapter 5, we describe the database model whose design is based on knowledge from Chapter 4. The database has a *Core* part for the regular text modules, an *Extension* part for the irregular document parts, a *Presentation* part for the XSL documents and a *Metadata* part with metadata information about the three other parts.

Chapter 6 presents a tutorial showing how to work with XML and XSL documents and how to view HTML documents in *RelAndXML*.

In Chapter 7, we explain the Java implementation of *RelAndXML*. We show how we connect the tree representation with the underlying XML document. Furthermore, we describe the assembling of XML documents from database tuples and their disassembling in fragments suitable for the database.

Finally, Chapter 8 concludes this thesis by briefly summarizing the results and by pointing out suggestions for future work.

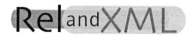

Figure 1.1: *RelAndXML* Logo

Chapter 2

The XML World – Introduction and Running Examples

This chapter gives an introduction to the XML world, providing an insight into the data format of the documents that are to be stored in *RelAndXML*. Later chapters will focus on *how* to store that data. The chapter contains a section about XML followed by a section about XSLT and XPath and a short section about XML query languages. The first section starts with introducing the metamarkup language XML itself, followed by a short historical overview. Subsequently, it is shown how context-free grammars for XML languages can be defined with Document Type Definitions (DTDs). XHTML, which has the same expressiveness as HTML, is presented as such an XML language. Thereafter, three types of XML documents are defined: data-centric, document-centric, and hypertext-centric. Graphs, the Document Object Model (DOM), and the Simple API for XML (SAX) are introduced as models for XML. The section ends with some running examples. The second section gives an introduction to the access of document parts with XPath, followed by an overview of XSLT, which is employed to write stylesheets for XML documents, and makes use of XPath expressions. Afterwards, some running examples are provided. As outlined in the specification for *RelAndXML* (see Section 1.2), the document order must be preserved when documents are saved as a collection of fragments. Therefore, we explain at several points in this chapter, how document order information can both be included and used in the XML and XSLT documents. The last section about XML query languages briefly introduces the evolving language XQuery and explains why SQL is used as query language for *RelAndXML*.

2.1 XML

2.1.1 Definition and Basic Concepts

XML – the eXtensible Markup Language – is a metamarkup language for text documents [XML00]. Data is represented as strings of text and is surrounded by markup describing the properties of the data. The markup occurs predominantly as *tags*, which are distinguished from the unmarked up text – the *character data* – by surrounding angle brackets "<" and ">". *Elements* are the basic building block of XML. An element begins with a *start tag* "<elementname>" and ends with an *end tag* "</elementname>" the difference being that it has an additional slash "/". Elements may contain character data and/or other elements, called *subelements*. Elements might also have *attributes* which consist of a name and a value. They are placed within the start tag in the form "<elementname attr='value'>". Several attributes are separated by whitespace; an element cannot have two attributes with the same name; single and double quotation marks can be used interchangeably. Elements with no content but possibly attributes are called *empty* and can be represented by a single *empty-element tag* that begins with "<" but ends with "/>". So, "<elementname attr='value'/>" is the short cut for "<elementname attr='value'></elementname>". An *XML document* has a single *root element*, which contains other elements and/or character data. A document has a natural order, called *document order*. In order to be processed by an XML parser or web browser, an XML document must be well-formed. To be *well-formed* it needs to have a hierarchical structure, also called tree structure, and to start with the *XML declaration*

```
<?xml version="1.0" encoding="ISO-8859-1"?>
```

The version number states the used XML specification, which is currently 1.0 (see also Subsection 2.1.2). XML uses the Unicode Standard [Uni03], where characters from all known languages are collected. To specify a subset, the attribute encoding is used (ISO-8859-1 is the encoding for most Western European languages).

The word "eXtensible" in XML hints at the fact that XML does not provide a fixed set of tags, instead XML is a metamarkup language allowing users to define their own XML markup languages.

Listing 2.1 shows a very short XML coded sample "Assignment 1". The well-formed document starts with the XML declaration in line 1, followed by the root element assignment in line 2. The assignment includes as attributes the user identifier uid, the version number, the date, and the boolean published. Subelements are number, dateOfIssue, deadline, and the element asHasQu ("assignment has question") leading to an encapsulated question. The question has uid, version, date and published as attributes and also the marks which can be achieved with a correct solution. In this first example, a question solely consists of a single paragraph element. The paragraph in turn consists of character data intermingled with a subelement emph. This compound is called *mixed content*.

Listing 2.1 XML coded "Assignment 1" (unpublished)

```
1   <?xml version="1.0" encoding="ISO-8859-1" ?>
2   <assignment uid="DB1_Su2002_A1" version="1.0"
3               published="false" date="06/14/02">
4       <number>Assignment 1</number>
5       <dateOfIssue>June 17, 2002</dateOfIssue>
6       <deadline>Monday, June 24, 2002, 4pm</deadline>
7       <asHasQu>
8           <question uid="DB1_Su2002_A1_Q1" version="1.0"
9                     published="false" date="06/07/02" marks="4">
10              <paragraph>
11                  Translate the <emph>Company</emph>
12                  ER schema into a relational schema.
13              </paragraph>
14          </question>
15      </asHasQu>
16  </assignment>
```

To distinguish between markup and character data, XML predefines five *entity references* for characters with markup-meaning that would cause problems in the document: the less-than sign < and the ampersand & must be used in element content. The others are optional. The greater-than sign > is allowed mostly for symmetry with <, since a greater-than sign cannot be misinterpreted as closing a tag. " (") and ' (') are used to include double resp. single quotation marks within double resp. single quotation marks.

When more than a few of these signs are used in a part of the document, this encoding becomes tedious. For that reason, a *CDATA section*, set off by a <![CDATA[and]]>, can be used; meaning everything in the section – except for the CDATA section end delimiter itself – is treated as raw character data, not markup. To include]]> within a CDATA section, one can write]]> .

Comments are enclosed by <!-- and --> and must not contain the string --. *Processing instructions* have the form <?*identifier* ... ?> and give information for applications processing the document. A widely used processing instruction, xml-stylesheet, is used to attach stylesheets to documents (see Subsection 2.2). Comments and processing instructions are allowed to appear anywhere in the document outside of a tag, particularly before or after the root element.

2.1.2   A Very Short History

XML is a descendant of SGML, which stands for Standard Generalized Markup Language. SGML is like XML a semantic and structural markup language for text documents; it has been an ISO-certified standard since 1986 [SGM86]. SGML is too powerful and complicated that it never became popular. SGML's biggest success was HTML, which is an SGML application. The current version is 4.01 [HTM99]. It provides a finite set of tags designed to describe web pages. HTML is so successful because of its simplicity. Otherwise, it mixes content, structure and layout, and provides no ways of integrating semantics with the data. Therefore, XML was designed as a subset of SGML retaining only the important features – like the separation of content, structure and layout of documents – with the aim to make XML simpler and more popular.

The World Wide Web Consortium (W3C) was created in October 1994 and has defined most of the important web standards [W3C03]. The specifications progress through several stages of maturity: Working Draft, Last Call Working Draft, Candidate Recommendation, Proposed Recommendation, and finally Recommendation.

XML version 1.0 was published as a W3C Recommendation in 1998; a second edition (still version 1.0) which corrects some minor errors was published in 2000 [XML00]. Currently, the W3C is working on XML 1.1, which got the status "Candidate Recommendation" in October 2002 [XML02]. XML 1.1 updates XML to use Unicode 3.1 and later versions. It also normalizes character encodings to ease string identity matching, indexing etc. (for example, "α" equals "α" in XML, but for a simple string algorithm they appear different). These improvements are not relevant for our work, furthermore most recent tools do not support this version yet; therefore XML 1.0 is used for *RelAndXML*. Seeing the benefits of XML, the W3C decided to define an XML-compatible version of HTML which is called XHTML [XHT02].

2.1.3   Document Type Definitions

As mentioned earlier, XML is a metamarkup language providing no fixed set of tags. But when XML is used to exchange data, individuals or organisations might better agree on a fixed set of tags – called *XML application* – for reasons of interoperability. This can be done by fixing a *schema*, which is a context-free grammar, that defines the XML application. The schema language defined in the XML 1.0 specification is the *document type definition* (DTD). A DTD describes which elements, attributes and entities may appear where in the document. We give an overview of the notation; for a full description, see the XML specification [XML00] or one of the many XML books, whereby [HM02] is recommended by the author.

Listing 2.2 shows a DTD for the unpublished "Assignment 1" in Listing 2.1; we call it *SmallCore* DTD. It has a number of entity, element and attribute declarations. Line 2

Listing 2.2 *SmallCore* DTD

```
1    <!-- Filename: smallcore.dtd -->
2    <!ENTITY % basic "uid CDATA #REQUIRED
3                      version CDATA #REQUIRED
4                      published (false | true) 'false'
5                      date CDATA #IMPLIED">
6    <!ELEMENT assignment (number, dateOfIssue?, deadline?, asHasQu+)>
7    <!ATTLIST assignment %basic;>
8    <!ELEMENT asHasQu (question)>
9    <!ATTLIST asHasQu ordinal CDATA #IMPLIED>
10   <!ELEMENT question (paragraph)>
11   <!ATTLIST question %basic;
12                      marks CDATA #IMPLIED>
13   <!ELEMENT number (#PCDATA)>
14   <!ELEMENT dateOfIssue (#PCDATA)>
15   <!ELEMENT deadline (#PCDATA)>
16   <!ELEMENT paragraph (#PCDATA | emph)*>
17   <!ELEMENT emph (#PCDATA)>
```

---

contains a *parameter entity declaration* which defines %basic; as short cut for the quoted string. This type of short cut can be used within the DTD and %basic; is used in attribute declarations (see below).

The *element declaration* in line 6 describes the assignment element. It states that each assignment element must contain a *sequence* of subelements: exactly one number element, zero or one dateOfIssue element(s) and zero or one deadline element(s) (suffix ?), followed by one or more asHasQu elements (suffix +). The sequence also fixes the order of the subelements. Another suffix is * for "zero or more of the element". The elements number, dateOfIssue and deadline may only contain *parsed character data* – plain text that might contain entity references –, but no subelements of any type. This is stated by the keyword #PCDATA. The element declaration paragraph in line 16 shows the only way to declare mixed content: #PCDATA must be the first in a list of *choices* (here just emph) and the choice can be made zero or more times. Elements can also be declared to have no content but possibly attributes (keyword EMPTY) or to have any content (keyword ANY), meaning they contain mixed content with any of the declared elements. (In particular, this means that ANY does NOT allow to write "anything".) The order of element declarations is not relevant, and the root element is not fixed within the DTD.

Attribute declarations describe the attributes of elements and have the keyword AT-TLIST. In line 7, the parameter entity of line 2 is used to define four attributes of the element assignment. The attributes uid and version are required, whereas the date is optional (keyword #IMPLIED). The type of uid, version and date is CDATA – this is the most general attribute type allowing any character data. The attribute published has an enumeration type with the values true or false; the literal false defines this value as default that is included by the XML parser if missing. The element asHasQu has an optional attribute ordinal, in which the desired ordinal number can be provided, when there are several questions on an assignment. The ordinal attribute is part of the document order information. Other attribute types are NMTOKEN, NMTOKENS, ENTITY, ENTITIES, ID, IDREF, IDREFS, and NOTATION.

General entity declarations are used to set short cuts that can be used within the XML document. The difference to the declaration of parsed entities is the missing % after the keyword ENTITY. The following line defines &oopj; as an abbreviation for "Object-oriented Programming with Java".

```
<!ENTITY oopj "Object-oriented Programming with Java">
```

A well-formed XML document including a *document type declaration* with an URL pointing to a DTD and conforming to that DTD is said to be *valid*. Accordingly, an *XML parser* which checks the conformity of an XML document with its DTD is called *validating*; it is called *non-validating* when it checks well-formedness only. We use Xerces, the validating XML parser of the Apache XML project [Xer03]. It can be used within Java applications (see Section 7.2). How to include a document type declaration, is shown in the following lines

```
1    <?xml version="1.0" encoding="ISO-8859-1" standalone="no">
2    <!DOCTYPE assignment SYSTEM "smallcore.dtd">
3    <assignment ...>
4        ...
5    </assignment>
```

which are to be added to the document in Listing 2.1. Line 1 contains the attribute standalone with value "no", stating that the XML document needs another file to be parsed. Line 2 says that the root element of the document is assignment and that the

DTD is found on the same machine (SYSTEM) in the same directory as the XML file (relative URL (*Uniform Resource Locator*)).

There are a number of W3C standardized XML applications like MathML, XHTML and so on. Their DTDs are publicly available and usually provided with the keyword PUBLIC and an absolute *Uniform Resource Identifier* (URI). A URI is either a URL or a *Uniform Resource Name* (URN), where a URN is an address agreed upon by an organization – it needs not exist. The above are examples for *external DTD*s; a DTD might also be included within the XML document (called *internal DTD*) or even be a combination of an *internal DTD subset* and an *external DTD subset*. The two subsets must be compatible. Neither can override the element declarations of the other. The following example combines the *SmallCore* DTD with the general entity declaration from above.

```
1    <?xml version="1.0" encoding="ISO-8859-1" standalone="no">
2    <!DOCTYPE assignment SYSTEM "smallcore.dtd" [
3            <!ENTITY oopj "Object-oriented Programming with Java">
4    ]>
```

An internal DTD can also be used to incorporate all HTML entities in a simple way. Why would one need HTML entities in XML? When the right encoding is chosen, e.g. ISO-8859-1 for German, all characters of the desired language are available for markup – for example <Straße>Höfchen</Straße> is well-formed XML – as well as for character data, and do not have to be written with entity references like ß or ö. But for every other character that is not in the chosen character set or not on the computer keyboard (e.g. greek characters and mathematical symbols often used in assignments), an entity declaration must provide the number of the character in the Unicode set. For example, the greek character α must be declared as <!ENTITY alpha "α">.

If more than a few HTML entities are used, it is easier to include all of them. The W3C provides three DTD fragments that together define all the familiar HTML character references. They can be included in an internal DTD as shown in Listing 2.3. However, it is recommendable to save local copies and to set the SYSTEM identifier accordingly, rather than downloading the DTD fragments every time a file is parsed.

One defining feature of *RelAndXML* is that it does not restrict the user with DTDs. We thought about providing the possibility to use internal DTDs to import such entity declarations, but that did not work since if entities are defined, elements have to be declared as well. See also page 92.

When a document includes tags from several DTDs, some tags might be defined multiple times, and for this reason, namespaces are useful. A *namespace* is a prefix to elements and attributes of the form *identifier:*. Each prefix is mapped to a URI by an xmlns:*prefix*

Listing 2.3 Internal DTD for including HTML entities

```
<!DOCTYPE assignment [
    <!ENTITY % xhtml-lat1 PUBLIC "-//W3C//ENTITIES Latin 1 for XHTML//EN"
            "http://www.w3.org/TR/xhtml1/DTD/xhtml-lat1.ent">
    <!ENTITY % xhtml-special PUBLIC "-//W3C//ENTITIES Special for XHTML//EN"
            "http://www.w3.org/TR/xhtml1/DTD/xhtml-special.ent">
    <!ENTITY % xhtml-symbol PUBLIC "-//W3C//ENTITIES Symbol for XHTML//EN"
            "http://www.w3.org/TR/xhtml1/DTD/xhtml-symbol.ent">
    %xhtml-lat1;
    %xhtml-special;
    %xhtml-symbol;
]>
```

---

attribute in the root element of the document. For an example, see Subsection 2.2.

The expressiveness of DTDs is rather limited. A DTD can neither describe the length or permitted values of the text content of elements, nor does it have knowledge of the standard data types like integer, double, etc. for attributes. To overcome these limitations, another schema language, called *XML Schema*, was standardized by the W3C. It has the advantage to be an XML language, so that schemas are written in XML instead of in some other notation like, for example, the DTD notation. XML Schema is more expressive, but usually results in lengthy schemas. The specification is so long that it was divided intro three parts [XMS01a, XMS01b, XMS01c]. Since XML Schema is not used for *RelAndXML*, we abstain from giving an introduction to it. There are numerous other XML schema languages including RELAX NG [REL03] and Schematron [Sch03a], each with their own strengths and weaknesses.

2.1.4   XHTML

XHTML is an XML application with the same vocabulary as HTML, so the differences between XHTML and HTML are minor. Since it has a DTD, XHTML forces to write HTML more correctly. Valid XHTML is displayed correctly only by newer browsers (Mozilla, Opera 5.0 and later, Internet Explorer 5.5 and later, as well as Netscape 6.0 and later). Older browsers have problems with processing instructions and CDATA sections, for instance. *RelAndXML* leaves the choice of HTML or XHTML as output format to the user. But XHTML has to be used for fragments to be included in XSLT stylesheets, since these are valid XML documents (see Section 2.2). Here is a list of the important differences:

- All tags are written in lower case, whereas in HTML lower and upper case might be mixed up.

- There must be an end tag for every start tag; e.g. </li> must not be omitted unlike in HTML. As a special case, HTML commands without end tag get an additional blank (to support older browser versions) and a slash like in <br /> or in <img src="myImage.gif" />.

- Attributes must have a quoted value, e.g. write <table border="1"> instead of <table border> and <select name="Options" multiple="multiple"> instead of <select name="Options" multiple>.

- Some commands are not allowed within others, for instance the "preformatted" command <pre> must not contain an image <img src="myImage.gif" />.

- The attribute name of the commands a, applet, form, frame, iframe, img, and map is replaced by id, e.g. <a id="myAnchor">...</a>.

- XHTML might contain CDATA sections and processing instructions.

Each XHTML document must contain a document type declaration, and there are three DTDs to choose from:

```
<!DOCTYPE html PUBLIC "-//W3C//DTD XHTML 1.0 Strict//EN"
          "http://www.w3.org/TR/xhtml1/DTD/xhtml1-strict.dtd">
```

The strict definition excludes all commands (elements and attributes) which are deprecated in HTML 4.01. This concerns many of the HTML commands used for presentation, such as the <font> tag and the align attribute – they have been replaced by the equivalent properties in the CSS (Cascading StyleSheet) model.

```
<!DOCTYPE html PUBLIC "-//W3C//DTD XHTML 1.0 Transitional//EN"
          "http://www.w3.org/TR/xhtml1/DTD/xhtml1-transitional.dtd">
```

The transitional DTD is closest to the HTML 4.01 standard and includes all the deprecated elements.

```
<!DOCTYPE html PUBLIC "-//W3C//DTD XHTML 1.0 Frameset//EN"
          "http://www.w3.org/TR/xhtml1/DTD/xhtml1-frameset.dtd">
```

The third DTD combines the transitional DTD with commands for frame sets.

The W3C published the XHTML standard as [XHT02] and offers a validation service for HTML and XHTML files at http://validator.w3.org/, where files can be uploaded and tested.

2.1.5 Document-centric versus Data-centric XML

XML was originally designed for the web, as an advanced version of HTML, to bring semantics into web pages – which means to write documents in the ordinary sense of the word. This type of document is called *document-centric*. It often has a rather irregular, frequently changing structure, lots of mixed content while the document order is essential. Other terms for this type are *semi-structured, document-oriented* and *document-processing-oriented* XML. Document-centric XML is of course well-formed, but often *non-valid* since it has no DTD (or other type of schema).

Compare the published version of "Assignment 1" (shown in Listing 2.4) to the *Small-Core* DTD in Listing 2.2 on page 11. It does not conform to this DTD because of the additional attribute folder in line 2, the decision to markup "Company" with the tag strong instead of with emph in line 10, the added keyword in lines 13-15, and the note about the exam in line 19. Please note that the comment in line 18 is included for further use of this example, whereas a DTD does neither restrict nor allow comments.

Listing 2.4 XML coded "Assignment 1" (published)

```
1    <assignment uid="DB1_Su2002_A1" version="1.0"
2                    published="true" date="06/14/02" folder="DB1_Su2002">
3        <number>Assignment 1</number>
4        <dateOfIssue>June 17, 2002</dateOfIssue>
5        <deadline>Monday, June 24, 2002, 4pm</deadline>
6        <asHasQu>
7          <question uid="DB1_Su2002_A1_Q1" version="1.0"
8                    published="true" date="06/07/02" marks="4">
9            <paragraph>
10               Translate the <strong>Company</strong>
11               ER schema into a relational schema.
12           </paragraph>
13           <keyword uid="ERschema" version="1.0" published="true">
14               <name>ER schema</name>
15           </keyword>
16         </question>
17       </asHasQu>
18       <!-- Add a question about 3NF here. -->
19       <exam>The exam is an <strong>open book</strong> exam.</exam>
20   </assignment>
```

Naturally, one could extend the *SmallCore* DTD to cover these additions. But if changes in the structure occur frequently, this becomes a strain to the DTD author.

A document-centric XML document is a string of text and all of its parts are therefore also strings. This is why DTDs (being the earliest schema definition language) do not describe data types. A more detailed description of documents is needed for *data-centric* XML. This type of XML is widely used for the exchange of data. Data-centric XML has sparse mixed content and the document order is usually unimportant. As mentioned earlier, a DTD (or XML Schema if data types shall be defined) is needed to exchange data sensibly, therefore data-centric XML is most of the time valid XML. Synonyms to data-centric XML are *data-oriented* as well as *data-processing-oriented* XML.

Listing 2.5 shows a data-centric XML document with data of a company[1]. A company has a number of departments, each having a number of employees. The order of the employee elements within a department element contains no semantic meaning.

Listing 2.5 Data-centric sample XML

```
<company>
    <department dnumber="5" dname="Research">
        <employee ssn="123456789">
            <fname>John</fname>
            <lname>Smith</lname>
        </employee>
        <employee ssn="453453453">
            <fname>Joyce</fname>
            <lname>English</lname>
        </employee>
    </department>
    <department dnumber="1" dname="Headquarters">
        <employee ssn="888665555">
            <fname>James</fname>
            <lname>Borg</lname>
        </employee>
    </department>
</company>
```

---

[1] A Company database, which contains this (and more) data, is one of the running examples for relational databases in [EN00].

2.1.6   Hypertext-centric XML

The distinction between data-centric and document-centric XML can be subtle, and some documents could be regarded either way. In hypertext application areas – where *RelAnd-XML* concentrates on – documents are written as a combination of new and existing text modules. Most of the text modules are data-centric, but their occurrence within the document is not very restricted and also, free text and markup might be allowed in between text modules. We see hypertext as mainly document-centric, but with data-centric parts and will use the term *hypertext-centric XML*.

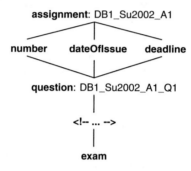

Figure 2.1: Hasse diagram for "Assignment 1"

The document order at large is important, but within the data-centric text modules it is sometimes dispensable. This imposes a partial order on the documents. Figure 2.1 shows a Hasse diagram for the published "Assignment 1". It states that number, dateOfIssue, and deadline might appear in any order, while the other items need to be ordered as follows: first question DB1_Su2002_A1_Q1, then the comment and at the end follows the note about the exam.

2.1.7   Graph Representation

XML documents are also represented as ordered and labeled directed graphs. XML elements are represented by nodes in the graph; nodes are labeled with identifiers. (We use system generated identifiers (sids) for this purpose.) Subelements are connected to their parent element with edges that are labeled by the name of the subelement. Attributes are connected to their element with dashed edges and comments with dotted edges. Values are shown as leaves in the graph. To represent the partial order, edges are labeled with their boxed ordinal number. The graph in Figure 2.2 corresponds to the published "Assignment 1" in Listing 2.4 on page 16 without most attributes.

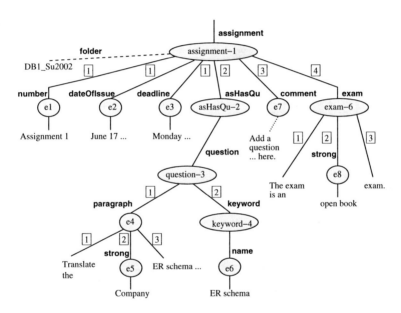

Figure 2.2: XML tree for "Assignment 1"

Listing 2.6 Running example "Assignment 1"

```
1     <assignment uid="DB1_Su2002_A1" version="1.0"
2                  published="true" date="06/14/02" folder="DB1_Su2002">
3        <number>Assignment 1</number>
4        <dateOfIssue>June 17, 2002</dateOfIssue>
5        <deadline>Monday, June 24, 2002, 4pm</deadline>
6        <asHasQu ordinal="2">
7           <question uid="DB1_Su2002_A1_Q1" version="1.0"
8                       published="true" date="06/07/02" marks="4">
9              <paragraph>
10                Translate the <strong>Company</strong>
11                ER schema into a relational schema.
12             </paragraph>
13             <keyword uid="ERschema" version="1.0" published="true">
14                <name>ER schema</name>
15             </keyword>
16          </question>
17       </asHasQu>
18       <comment ordinal="3">
19          <!-- Add a question about 3NF here. -->
20       </comment>
21       <exam ordinal="4">
22          <text ordinal="1">The exam is an</text>
23          <strong ordinal="2">open book</strong>
24          <text ordinal="3">exam.</text>
25       </exam>
26    </assignment>
```

To integrate the ordering information into the XML document we use the attribute ordinal and wrap the character data in mixed content parts with the element text and comments with the element comment. Listing 2.6 shows the comment and the exam element at the end of "Assignment 1" with wrapping and ordinal attributes; we will use this version of "Assignment 1" as running example.

There are several possibilities to define links in between and across XML documents (like the attribute types ID, IDREF(S) in DTDs, as well as XLink and XPointer) justifying the used term "graph" for XML documents. Since references can be represented as regular edges, so that the graph can be reduced to a tree, we use the term *XML tree* in the subsequent chapters.

The graph presentation is one of several data models for XML, some others are described in the next subsection.

2.1.8 DOM and SAX

The *Document Object Model* (DOM) is a programming language-neutral object model, standardized by the W3C [DOM03]; it defines the logical structure of documents and the way a document is accessed and manipulated, by providing a tree-based Application Programming Interface (API) to process those documents. The DOM Core module contains the tree model; the definition of the DOM interface (DOM API) is written with the Interface Definition Language (IDL), which is the specification language of the CORBA standard [COR03]. Since Java is used in this thesis, we write interfaces and methods with the notation from the Java binding [DJL00]. The root of the class hierarchy in the DOM Core is the Node interface. It can be used to extract information from any DOM object without knowing its actual type. The Node interface provides methods to navigate and manipulate the graph structure, e.g. getParent(), getChildren(), getNextSibling(), and removeChild(Node). The class hierarchy of the DOM is shown in Figure 2.3. It includes subclasses like Document for the document's root, Element for elements, Attr for attributes, etc. Each of these classes contains methods to access the represented XML construct.

The *Simple API for XML* (SAX) is another object model for XML, which is public-domain software and not standardized by the W3C [SAX03], but as popular as the DOM. Whereas DOM is a tree-based model, SAX does not build a complete parse tree at the beginning of processing, but gives events to the application program, e.g. when a start or end tag is found.

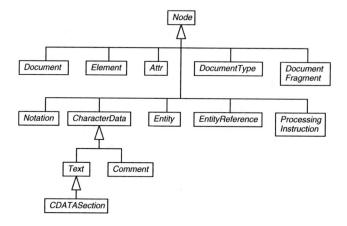

Figure 2.3: DOM Class Hierarchy

XML 1.0, DOM, SAX, XML Schema, XPath and XQuery all have similar but subtly different conceptual models of the structure of an XML document. For instance, the XPath and XQuery data models do not contain CDATA sections, entity references, and document type declarations. Thus the W3C provides in the *XML Information Set* (also called *XML Infoset*) a consistent set of definitions for use in the other specifications that refer to the information in a well-formed XML document [XIn01].

2.1.9 Running Examples

Apart from "Assignment 1" in Listing 2.6 we use four more XML documents as running examples in this thesis. Listing 2.7 shows "Assignment 2", which contains two questions. The asHasQu elements have ordinal attributes that allow to derive the right order of the questions. This XML document is valid to the *SmallCore* DTD.

Listing 2.7 XML running example "Assignment 2"

```
1    <assignment uid="A2">
2        <number>Assignment 2</number>
3        <dateOfIssue>October 14, 2002</dateOfIssue>
4        <deadline>Monday, October 21, 2002, 4pm</deadline>
5        <asHasQu ordinal="2">
6            <question uid="Q2">
7                <paragraph>Prove <emph>Lemma</emph> 2.2.</paragraph>
8            </question>
9        </asHasQu>
10        <asHasQu ordinal="1">
11            <question uid="Q1">
12                <paragraph>Prove <emph>Lemma</emph> 2.1.</paragraph>
13            </question>
14        </asHasQu>
15    </assignment>
```

Assignment 2 contains questions but no course information, in Assignment 3, this is vice versa; see Listing 2.8. This split will help to keep the examples in the following chapters short.

Another example is "Question 4", which is part of "Assignment 4", shown in Listing 2.9 on the following page. In HTML, its text reads "Solve question 2 of assignment 2 by using question 1 and Theorem 3 in the lecture notes" and is divided into a paragraph element, two links and two text elements, all of these having ordinal attributes. The first link points to a question in another assignment and the second to a question of the same assignment. Both links have the attribute internal="true", which means that they link to another document or object within *RelAndXML*. The question element has an uid identifier and its subelements have sid identifiers.

Listing 2.10 shows XML code for "Question 5" which contains data for a figure of an ER schema, with attributes like height and width. Since it was drawn with the Unix program *xfig* (sourcetype), it has a sourcefilename.

Listing 2.8 XML running example "Assignment 3"

```
1    <assignment uid="A3" version="1.0" published="false">
2        <number>Assignment 3</number>
3        <dateOfIssue>October 21, 2002</dateOfIssue>
4        <deadline>Monday, October 28, 2002, 4pm</deadline>
5        <isAssignmentOfCourse>
6            <course uid="FCS1" version="1.0">
7                <name>Fundamentals of Computer Science 1</name>
8                <semester>Winter 2002/03</semester>
9            </course>
10       </isAssignmentOfCourse>
11   </assignment>
```

Listing 2.9 XML running example "Question 4"

```
1    <assignment uid="A4">
2        <number>Assignment 4</number>
3        <asHasQu ordinal="1">
4            <question uid="Q3" marks="4">
5                <paragraph>Prove Lemma 3.1.</paragraph>
6            </question>
7        </asHasQu>
8        <asHasQu ordinal="2">
9            <question uid="Q4">
10               <paragraph sid="P1" ordinal="1">Solve</paragraph>
11               <link sid="L1" ordinal="2" internal="true">
12                   <href>A2.html#Q2</href>
13                   <text>question 2 of assignment 2</text>
14               </link>
15               <link sid="L2" ordinal="4" internal="true">
16                   <href>#Q3</href>
17                   <text>question 1</text>
18               </link>
19               <text sid="T2" ordinal="3">by using</text>
20               <text sid="T4" ordinal="5">
21                   and Theorem 3 in the lecture notes.</text>
22           </question>
23       </asHasQu>
24   </assignment>
```

Listing 2.10 Running example "Question 5"

```
1   <question sid="Q5" uid="Question5" marks="6">
2       <paragraph>Transform the shown ER schema into a relational schema.
3       </paragraph>
4       <figure date='June 2002' published='true'
5               uid='Figure_Company_ER' version='1.0'>
6           <filename>company_ERschema.gif</filename>
7           <height>131</height>
8           <width>226</width>
9           <type>gif</type>
10          <sourcefilename>company_ERschema.fig</sourcefilename>
11          <sourcetype>xfig</sourcetype>
12      </figure>
13  </question>
```

2.2   XSLT and XPath

XSLT, the *eXtensible Stylesheet Language for Transformations*, has been a W3C Recommendation since 1999 [XSL99]. XSLT is an XML application, which means that XSLT stylesheets are written in XML notation. XPath, the *XML Path Language* [XPa99], is used within stylesheets to describe sets of XML nodes. The *eXtensible Stylesheet Language* (XSL) consists of XSLT, XPath, and the *XSL Formatting Objects* (XSL-FO), which allow to define a sophisticated page layout [XSL03]. Formatting objects are not used in this thesis.

An *XSL processor* takes an XML document and an XSLT stylesheet as input documents to produce an output document. For processing, the XML document is seen as XML tree. The XSL processor starts at the root and selects a matching rule. This rule includes information which nodes are to be processed next. This means in particular that the processing order is not restricted to the document order of the input XML document. We use Xalan, the XSL processor of the Apache XML project [Xal03]. It can be used as a command line tool or within Java applications (see Section 7.2).

In the following, we describe enough XSLT and XPath to read the running examples and to judge the way XSLT is saved in Chapter 5; but considering the rich possibilities of these languages we will not give more than a short introduction. Apart from the official documents [XSL99, XPa99], there are many books on this topic – a good overview is given in [HM02], and detailed references can be found in [Kay01] and [Tid01].

2.2.1   Basic XPath Concepts

XPath is a language for specifying navigation within an XML document and for identifying parts of the XML document. XPath views an XML document as a tree of nodes very similar to a DOM tree, except for that in XPath there are only seven kinds of nodes: the root node as well as element, attribute, text, comment, processing instruction, and namespace nodes. This means especially that the XML declaration and the document type declaration are not included in XPath's view of an XML document. Also, all entity references and CDATA sections are resolved.

The result of evaluating an XPath expression on a given XML document is a set of nodes sorted according to document order. A *location path* expression is built of successive *location steps*, which are separated by forward slashes. Each location step is evaluated relative to a particular node in the document called the *context node*.

The simplest location paths and steps are the following. The forward slash / selects the root node of the document. A single element name *name* selects all child elements of the context node with the specified name. The asterisk * is a wildcard matching any element node regardless of name. This is analogous for attributes: @*name* selects all attributes of the context node with the specified name and @* matches any attribute node.

In general, each location step contains an axis and a node test separated by a double colon. It might be suffixed with one or more predicates enclosed in square brackets that further reduce the node set.

```
location-step  ::= axis::node-test[predicate]
```

All of these parts are optional, since there is also some abbreviated syntax (see below). The most common axes are the child, parent, self, attribute, and descendant-or-self axes. There are node tests for text nodes (text()), comment nodes (comment()), processing instructions (processing-instruction()), and all kinds of nodes (node()).

Some very common location steps have an abbreviated syntax for axis:: like shown in the following table. Only the abbreviated syntax is allowed in XSLT match patterns (see below).

Location Step	Abbreviation	Explanation
child::*name*	*name*	the child element *name*
self::*	.	the context node
parent::*	..	the parent node
attribute::*name*	@*name*	the attribute *name*
/descendant-or-self::node()/	//	any descendant of the context node or the context node itself

Predicates contain a Boolean expression, which is tested for each node in the context node list. There are some built-in functions, which can be used in predicates (and in expressions). For instance, position() returns the position of the current node in the context node set.

Multiple location paths can be combined with the union operator | to get the union of the node sets retrieved by the location paths.

We conclude this subsection with a few XPath expression examples. For more examples, see the match patterns in the following subsection.

Expression	matches
//question	all question elements in the document
@uid	the uid attribute of the context node
//question[@published='true']	all questions that are published
//question/paragraph	the paragraphs of all questions
//text()[.='Test']	all text nodes with value Test

2.2.2 Basic XSLT Concepts

A well-formed XSLT document contains the XML declaration and an xsl:stylesheet element (or the synonym xsl:transform) as root.

```
<?xml version="1.0" encoding="ISO-8859-1"?>
<xsl:stylesheet version="1.0" xmlns:xsl="http://www.w3.org/1999/XSL/Transform">
    . . .
</xsl:stylesheet>
```

The attribute xmlns:xsl declares the namespace xsl: for the document. This protects against mixing up XSLT tags with tags from the XML document to be transformed. Next is usually the description of the output format with the <xsl:output ... /> command. The method attribute specifies the type of the output ("xml", "html", or "text"). The methods "xml" and "html" can be further described with the version and the document type dec-laration (attributes doctype-public and doctype-system). If the attribute indent is set to "yes", the XSLT parser breaks the lines of the output document more or less sensibly, whereas everything is written on a single line when indent equals "no". The two following examples show an xsl:output command for HTML and for XHTML respectively.

```
<xsl:output method="html" version="4.01" encoding="ISO-8859-1"
    indent="yes" media-type="text/html"
    doctype-public="-//W3C//DTD HTML 4.01 Transitional//EN"
    doctype-system="http://www.w3.org/TR/1999/REC-html401-19991224/loose.dtd"/>

<xsl:output method="xml" version="1.0" encoding="ISO-8859-1"
    indent="yes" media-type="text/xml"
    doctype-public="-//W3C//DTD XHTML 1.0 Transitional//EN"
    doctype-system="http://www.w3.org/TR/xhtml1/DTD/xhtml1-transitional.dtd"/>
```

XSLT contains template rules that are applied to the nodes in the XML document. Each template rule has an XPath pattern describing the nodes the rule should be applied to and a number of templates. The XML element is called xsl:template and has four attributes as the following lines show.

```
<xsl:template match = pattern
            name = qname
            priority = number
            mode = qname>
    <!-- some templates -->
</xsl:template>
```

The attribute match defines the pattern with an XPath expression. The simplest ex-ample for this is just an element name like "question". As an alternative to a pattern, a template rule can be given a name. Using this attribute, a template rule can be called independently of some node structure. The attributes priority and mode are used to define several template rules for the same pattern. When the pattern matches, the attribute values determine which template rule is to be called.

The processing instruction xml:stylesheet can be used to attach a stylesheet to an XML document. It must be included in the prolog of the document and contains either an absolute or a relative URL to the stylesheet file, see the following lines.

```
<?xml version="1.0" encoding="ISO-8859-1" ?>
<?xml-stylesheet type="application/xml" href="assignment.xsl" ?>
<assignment ... >
    . . .
</assignment>
```

A choice of templates

Templates build the body of a template rule together with text and tags that are directly copied to the output. There are a number of templates available.

```
<xsl:value-of select = pattern />
```
The value-of template returns the value of the node selected by the pattern. The value of an element is its text content stripped of any tags and with entity and character references resolved.

```
<xsl:apply-templates select = pattern mode=qname />
```
This template selects all the nodes matching the pattern for processing. For each node, the XSL processor selects a matching template rule (taking the optional mode into account) and moves on to that rule. In particular, this might change the order of traversal.

```
<xsl:apply-templates />
```
This template processes all child nodes of the current node using preorder traversal.

The following list shows some other templates and their purpose.

- xsl:text for the insertion of text, especially blanks

- xsl:for-each for iteration loops

- xsl:if, xsl:choose, xsl:when, and xsl:otherwise for conditional processing

- xsl:copy for copying elements and xsl:copy-of for copying tree fragments

- xsl:sort for sorting

For some of these, there are examples in Subsection 2.2.3.

The following lines show an example with two template rules for question and paragraph.

```
<xsl:template match="question">
    <h4>Marks: <xsl:value-of select="@marks"/></h4>
    <xsl:apply-templates select="paragraph"/>
</xsl:template>

<xsl:template match="paragraph">
    <p><xsl:apply-templates/></p>
</xsl:template>
```

In the question rule, the marks of the question are output as an HTML heading <h4>. Then the template rule for paragraph is called. The paragraph rule puts all its content into an HTML paragraph <p>.

Built-In Template Rules

What will happen in the previous example, if there are no template rules for @marks and for an emph subelement of paragraph? XSLT provides default built-in template rules for the different kinds of nodes, which are applied if no specific template rule is available in a stylesheet. For text and attribute nodes, the built-in template rule copies their value into the output document. Be aware though that attribute nodes are only processed, when a template rule asks for it. If there is no specific template rule for the corresponding element, the attribute content will not be displayed. The default template rule for the root node and for element nodes processes all child nodes by preorder traversal. For comments and processing instructions the built-in template rule says not to output anything into the result tree.

```
<xsl:template match="text()|@*">
    <xsl:value-of select="."/>
</xsl:template>

<xsl:template match="*|/">
    <xsl:apply-templates/>
</xsl:template>

<xsl:template match="processing-instruction()|comment()"/>
```

2.2.3   Running Examples

In the following examples, we are especially interested in ordering, sorting and numbering elements.

The simplest way of changing the order of elements is writing the templates in the desired order.

```
<xsl:template match="assignment[@uid='A2']">
    <xsl:apply-templates select="asHasQu/question[@uid='Q1']"/>
    <xsl:apply-templates select="asHasQu/question[@uid='Q2']"/>
</xsl:template>
```

The shown template rule for "Assignment 2" (see Listing 2.7) calls a template rule for question "Q1" before calling one for question "Q2". There might be two different template rules for the questions, but there might be just one template rule as well. This approach has the disadvantage that a stylesheet must be written for each assignment.

A more general approach is possible because "Assignment 2" contains ordinal attributes; it is shown in the following lines.

```
1   <xsl:for-each select='asHasQu'>
2       <xsl:sort select='@ordinal' data-type='number'/>
3       <h3><a id="question/@uid"/>
4           Question <xsl:number value="position()" /></h3>
5       <xsl:apply-templates select="question"/>
6   </xsl:for-each>
```

The xsl:for-each command loops over all asHasQu elements, but before the loop is started, the xsl:sort command is executed. It sorts the asHasQu elements by their ordinal attribute using the data type number (number sorts the values 2, 1, 10 as 1, 2, 10 whereas the default value text sorts them as 1, 10, 2). In the third line, an HTML anchor is generated. In line 4 the xsl:number command outputs the number of each question on this assignment as "Question 1", "Question 2" and so on, using the XPath expression position() which returns the position of a node between its siblings. Afterwards the question rule is called.

Listing 2.11 shows the complete stylesheet for the XML running examples "Assignment 1" and "Assignment 2". It has templates for assignment, question, paragraph, exam, text, and strong. The keywords of the question are seen as an aid for the author of the assigment only and are not printed on the assignment.

The complete HTML output for "Assignment 1" is shown in Listing 2.12, and the body of the HTML document for "Assignment 2" in Listing 2.13. Since there is no template rule for emph, the built-in template rule for elements is used. For completeness, the XSL templates and the HTML output for "Assignment 3", "Question 4" and "Question 5" are shown in the Listings 2.14 to 2.19.

Listing 2.11 XSL stylesheet for "Assignment 1" and "Assignment 2"

```
1    <?xml version="1.0" encoding="ISO-8859-1"?>
2    <xsl:stylesheet version="1.0" xmlns:xsl="http://www.w3.org/1999/XSL/Transform">
3
4    <xsl:output method="html" version="4.01" encoding="ISO-8859-1"
5        indent="yes" media-type="text/html"
6        doctype-public="-//W3C//DTD HTML 4.01 Transitional//EN"
7        doctype-system="http://www.w3.org/TR/1999/REC-html401-19991224/loose.dtd"/>
8
9    <xsl:template match="assignment">
10   <html>
11   <head> <title><xsl:value-of select="number"/></title> </head>
12   <body>
13   <h1><xsl:value-of select='number'/>
14       <xsl:if test='dateOfIssue'>- <xsl:value-of select='dateOfIssue'/></xsl:if>
15   </h1>
16   <xsl:if test='deadline'>
17       <h2>Deadline: <xsl:value-of select='deadline'/></h2>
18   </xsl:if>
19       <xsl:for-each select="asHasQu">
20       <xsl:sort select='@ordinal' data-type='number'/>
21           <h3><a id="question/@uid"/>
22               Question <xsl:number value="position()" /></h3>
23           <xsl:apply-templates select="question"/>
24       </xsl:for-each>
25       <hr />
26       <xsl:apply-templates select="exam"/>
27   </body>
28   </html>
29   </xsl:template>
30
31   <xsl:template match="question">
32       <h4>Marks: <xsl:value-of select="@marks"/></h4>
33       <xsl:apply-templates select="paragraph"/>
34   </xsl:template>
35
36   <xsl:template match="paragraph">
37       <p><xsl:apply-templates/></p>
38   </xsl:template>
39
40   <xsl:template match="exam">
41       <p><i>Note:</i><xsl:apply-templates>
42           <xsl:sort select="@ordinal" data-type="number"/>
43       </xsl:apply-templates></p>
44   </xsl:template>
45
46   <xsl:template match='text'>
47       <xsl:text> </xsl:text><xsl:apply-templates/><xsl:text> </xsl:text>
48   </xsl:template>
49
50   <xsl:template match="strong">
51       <strong><xsl:apply-templates/></strong>
52   </xsl:template>
53
54   </xsl:stylesheet>
```

Listing 2.12 HTML output for "Assignment 1"

```
<!DOCTYPE HTML PUBLIC "-//W3C//DTD HTML 4.01 Transitional//EN"
        "http://www.w3.org/TR/1999/REC-html401-19991224/loose.dtd">
<html>
<head>
    <META http-equiv="Content-Type" content="text/html; charset=ISO-8859-1">
    <title>Assignment 1</title>
</head>
<body>
    <h1>Assignment 1 - June 17, 2002</h1>
    <h2>Deadline: Monday, June 24, 2002, 4pm</h2>
    <h3><a id="DB1_Su2002_A1_Q1"></a>Question 1</h3>
    <h4>Marks: 4</h4>
    <p>Translate the <strong>Company</strong>
            ER schema into a relational schema. </p>
    <hr>
    <p><i>Note:</i> The exam is an <strong>open book</strong> exam.</p>
</body>
</html>
```

Listing 2.13 HTML output for "Assignment 2"

```
<body>
    <h1>Assignment 2</h1>
    <h3><a id="Q1">Question 1</a></h3>
    <h4>Marks: 4</h4>
    <p>Prove Lemma 2.1.</p>
    <h3><a id="Q2">Question 2</a></h3>
    <h4>Marks: 4</h4>
    <p>Prove Lemma 2.2.</p>
    <hr>
</body>
```

Listing 2.14 XSL templates for "Assignment 3"

```
<xsl:template match='assignment'>
    ...
    <xsl:if test='isAssignmentOfCourse'>
    <h2><xsl:apply-templates select='isAssignmentOfCourse/course'/></h2>
    </xsl:if>
    ...
</xsl:template>
<xsl:template match='course'>
    <xsl:value-of select='name'/><xsl:text> - </xsl:text>
    <xsl:value-of select='semester'/>
</xsl:template>
```

Listing 2.15 HTML output for "Assignment 3"

```
<body>
    <h1>Assignment 3 - October 21, 2002</h1>
    <h2>Fundamentals of Computer Science 1 - Winter 2002/03</h2>
    <h2>Deadline: Monday, October 28, 2002, 4pm</h2>
</body>
```

Listing 2.16 XSL templates for "Question 4"

```
<xsl:template match='question[@uid="Question4"]'>
    <h4>Marks: <xsl:value-of select='@marks'/></h4>
    <xsl:apply-templates mode='extended'>
        <xsl:sort select='@ordinal' data-type='number'/>
    </xsl:apply-templates>
</xsl:template>

<xsl:template match='paragraph' mode='extended'>
    <xsl:apply-templates/><xsl:text> </xsl:text>
</xsl:template>

<xsl:template match='link' mode='extended'>
    <xsl:text> </xsl:text>
    <a href="{href}"><xsl:value-of select='text'/></a><xsl:text> </xsl:text>
</xsl:template>

<xsl:template match='text' mode='extended'>
    <xsl:text> </xsl:text><xsl:apply-templates/><xsl:text> </xsl:text>
</xsl:template>
```

Listing 2.17 HTML output for "Question 4"

```
Solve
<a href="A2.html#Q2">question 2 of assignment 2</a>
by using
<a href="#Q3">question 1</a>
and Theorem 3 in the lecture notes.
```

Listing 2.18 XSL templates for "Question 5"

```
<xsl:template match='question[@uid="Question5"]'>
    <h4>Marks: <xsl:value-of select='@marks'/></h4>
    <xsl:apply-templates select="paragraph"/>
    <xsl:apply-templates select="figure"/>
</xsl:template>

<xsl:template match='figure'>
    <img src="{filename}" alt="{@uid}"
            width="{width}" height="{height}"/>
</xsl:template>
```

Listing 2.19 HTML output for "Question 5"

```
<p>Transform the shown ER schema into a relational schema.</p>
<img height="131" width="226"
        alt="Figure_Company_ER"
        src="company_ERschema.gif">
```

2.3 XML Query Languages

The XML Query Working Group of the W3C has been working on a standardized query language for XML since 1998, but the specification of *XQuery* still has the stage Working Draft [XQu03].

Commercial XML database systems (see Chapter 3) mostly use XPath with extensions for queries over multiple documents. Research groups often preferred XML-QL [XQL98] during the last years, but there are also numerous proprietary query languages for XML.

During the design phase and the implementation of *RelAndXML*, the possible outcome of the XML Query Working Group was still very unclear. Furthermore, the availability of an implementation of the query language was unclear. The usual way for researchers was to write their own translator from the preferred XML query language to the query language of the chosen database, for instance to SQL for a relational database [TVB+02, YASU01]. Since the implementation of such a translator is a project of its own, we decided that the use of an XML query language is out of the scope of the project *RelAndXML*. We use SQL to query the data in *RelAndXML*.

In the future, XQuery will most probably be the most popular XML query language. Many XML database vendors have already implemented some version of XQuery. The current version of XQuery and a list of implementations can be found at [XMQ03]. If we implement an add-on for *RelAndXML* in the future, it will use XQuery. We give a very brief introduction in the following.

XQuery is a query language for XML documents and collections of these documents. It is an extension of XPath 2.0, which means that (almost) every XPath expression is an XQuery expression. XQuery uses the same data model as XPath, so it has the same seven kinds of nodes: document, element, attribute, text, namespace, processing instruction, and comment. It is a functional language: each expression operates on instances of the data model and produces an instance of the data model.

The FLWR expression (say "flower") is as central to XQuery as SELECT is to SQL. It consists of one or more FOR and/or LET clauses, an optional WHERE clause, and a RETURN clause.

The FOR and LET clauses bind variables differently as the following examples show. The result of the XQuery expression

```
LET $i := (<one/>, <two/>)
RETURN <r>{$i}</r>
```

is   `<r><one/><two/></r>`. The result of

```
FOR $i := (<one/>, <two/>)
RETURN <r>{$i}</r>
```

is `<r><one/></r><r><two/></r>`. The WHERE clause filters the tuples selected in the LET and FOR clauses. The RETURN clause generates an XML fragment for every tuple in the result.

Joins are very similar to SQL joins. The following query shows a join that selects pairs of assignments and questions whose author is the same. The FOR clause selects all assignment and question fragments in the queried document and the WHERE clause filters these fragments leaving only those, where the author is the same. The RETURN clause creates an element `<sameauthor>` for each pair, with attributes for the author and the user identifiers of the assignment and the question.

```
FOR $a IN //assignment, $q IN //question
WHERE $a/@author = $q/@author
RETURN <sameauthor author={$a/@author}
            assignment={$a/@uid} question={$a/@uid}></sameauthor>
```

For more information on XQuery, see for example [EM02a] or [Sch03b].

2.4   Summary: RelAndXML's World

In this chapter, we gave an introduction to the XML world which is based on XML and DTDs. XML documents can now be classified in data-centric, document-centric and hypertext-centric documents. *RelAndXML* is designed for hypertext-centric documents, which contain structured, data-centric text modules as well as unstructured, document-centric parts. Graphs, DOM and SAX can be used as data models for XML. We use XSLT and XPath to convert XML documents to the output language HTML or XHTML. The chapter contains running examples for XML, XSLT and HTML that are used in the following chapters. XML query languages are out of the scope of this thesis. We use SQL to query the data in *RelAndXML*.

Chapter 3

Selecting a Database System for RelAndXML

The aim of this chapter is the selection of a suitable database type for the system *RelAnd-XML* without introducing a dependency on a single DBMS product. In the first section, we introduce three types of XML databases. The second section contains an overview of the various data models which are in use for XML databases and lists some of the products built on these data models together with their XML database type. We also explain why we decided on using an object-relational DBMS for *RelAndXML*. In the third section, we describe various features of the SQL standard and list which of them are implemented in the most popular object-relational DBMSs. We concentrate on features that we considered using for *RelAndXML* and which influenced our decision for a particular ORDBMS. Furthermore, we describe the new SQL/XML part of the SQL standard, which will most probably be published in 2003, and the quite different current XML extensions of the most popular ORDBMSs. The final section summarizes the decision to implement *RelAndXML* as middleware on an object-relational DBMS.

3.1 Types of XML Databases

A general definition for an XML database is the following.

> An XML database is a collection of XML documents that persist and can be manipulated. [Gra02]

The *Initiative for XML Databases* XML:DB has defined three different types of XML databases [XDB03]: *native XML database*, *XML enabled database*, and *hybrid XML database*. The definitions are as follows.

Native XML Database (NXD)

(a) Defines a (logical) model for an XML document – as opposed to the data in that document – and stores and retrieves documents according to that model. At a minimum, the model must include elements, attributes, PCDATA, and document order. Examples of such models are the XPath data model, the XML Infoset, and the models implied by the DOM and the events in SAX 1.0.

(b) Has an XML document as its fundamental unit of (logical) storage, just as a relational database has a row in a table as its fundamental unit of (logical) storage.

(c) Is not required to have any particular underlying data model. For example, it can be built on a relational, hierarchical, or object-oriented database, or use a proprietary storage format such as indexed, compressed files.

XML Enabled Database (XEDB)   – A database that has an added XML mapping layer provided either by the database vendor or a third party. This mapping layer manages the storage and retrieval of XML data. Data that is mapped into the database is mapped into application specific formats and the original XML meta-data and structure may be lost. Data retrieved as XML is NOT guaranteed to have originated in XML form. Data manipulation may occur via either XML specific technologies (e.g. XPath, XSL-T, DOM or SAX) or other database technologies (e.g. SQL). The fundamental unit of storage in an XEDB is implementation dependent. [...]

Hybrid XML Database (HXD)   – A database that can be treated as either a Native XML Database or as an XML Enabled Database depending on the requirements of the application. [...]

XML documents can also be stored in databases via middleware.

Middleware   – Software that is called from an application to transfer data between XML documents and databases. In general, it does not require the database to have any XML features.

All of the above databases might be combined with a web server. Therefore, we add the following definition.

Web Database System   – A Web database system is a database system that delivers persistent data via the Web [Gra02]. Apart from a usual database system it includes a Web server and network protocols.

Native XML databases are not suitable for *RelAndXML*, since their fundamental unit of storage is an XML document, and *RelAndXML* is designed to save fragments of XML documents. An XML enabled database is only suitable for *RelAndXML*, if it does preserve the original XML metadata and structure like comments, CDATA sections, processing instructions, and document order. Hybrid XML databases or middleware are most appropriate for the hypertext-centric XML we want to store in our system. In this way, we can combine features of XML enabled databases for the text modules with features of native XML databases for the additional parts like comments and free markup or free text. How to combine these features is a main topic of this thesis. Since *RelAndXML* will not include a web server, it is not a web database system.

3.2 XML Databases with Various Data Models

In this section, we give an overview of the various data models of XML databases and the corresponding storage techniques. We also name a few commercial or open-source products built on these models and assign XML database types to them. Note that there is a fast-moving market for XML databases. Bourret maintains a regularly updated list of XML database products at [Bou03b].

3.2.1   File Systems

XML documents can be stored and managed simply as files in a file system; the fundamental unit of storage are the complete XML documents. The advantage of a file system is that it is easy to maintain. XSLT and XQuery can be used to search for documents. A web server can also be added. Storing and loading documents is very fast, since there is no transformation needed at all. Even though this is an XML database in the sense of the general definition of [Gra02], the disadvantages of a file system are that the main benefits of DBMSs are missing: data security, query languages, concurrency control, and recovery facilities. Nevertheless, managing XML documents with the file system is reasonable when the following criteria apply:

- there is a relatively small number of documents

- the documents are small enough to be worked on in main memory

- there is single user operation

A file system is not suitable for *RelAndXML*, since we need a smaller fundamental unit of storage than complete XML documents.

3.2.2   Object-Oriented Database Systems

There are two ways of mapping XML to an object-oriented database system, the object-centric approach for data-centric documents and the node-centric approach for document-centric XML. For the *object-centric approach*, an object-oriented class model is generated from the DTD and used as database schema. XML documents are then seen as objects within the class model.[1] The *node-centric approach* is based on building a class hierarchy on the W3C DOM objects Attr, CharacterData, Comment, Document, Element, and Node. In this way, any document can be saved. Since each document is shredded to many small objects, it is very important that these are stored very efficiently.

The object-oriented database management system POET offers a middleware component which is able to store XML with the object-centric or the node-centric approach. POET is a hybrid XML database [POE03].

The eXtensible Information Server (XIS) of eXcelon [eXc03] is a web-enabled native XML database that is built on the company's own object-oriented database management system ObjectStore. It manages XML using the node-centric approach and comes with a DOM and XQL interface, an XML parser, an XSLT engine as well as XQuery support. The fundamental unit of storage are complete documents, which means that documents are retrieved in their entirety, and that there is no exploration or browsing of the contents of a document.

We could have used an object-oriented database for *RelAndXML*, but decided against it for the following reasons. In [Heu02], Heuer argues that the object-oriented DBMS standard by the ODMG (Object Database Management Group) is weak, inconsistent, and lacks some DBMS functionality like access authorization and views and that object-oriented DBMS products only have a niche at the market. But there will be no future versions of the ODMG standard, since as quoted from [ODM03] "The ODMG group completed its work on object data management standards in 2001 and was disbanded." Furthermore, there seems to be less interest in the research community for object-oriented databases than for (object-)relational databases: For example, the well-known online computer science bibliography DBLP (see [DBL03]) lists 11 papers for the search "XML object-oriented", but 77 for the search "XML relational" (both considering all years). The papers with "object-oriented database" in the title decrease each year (51 in 1999, 40

---

[1]This approach works analogously to the *object-relational mapping* described in Subsection 4.1.2 on page 65. Instead of foreign key relationships between tables, we get associations between classes.

in 2000, 32 in 2001, 26 in 2002), whereas the number of papers with "relational database" in the title is fairly constant (54 in 1999, 56 in 2000, 58 in 2001, 54 in 2002). Note that the result sets for the term "relational" also contain the term "object-relational".

3.2.3 Proprietary Storage Formats

Proprietary storage formats are used by most of the native XML databases. They can be based on knowledge from hierarchical, object-oriented, or object-relational DBMSs and/or use information retrieval methods on indexed, compressed files. In order to keep their proprietary storage formats as internal knowledge, the companies of most products give only very little information. Some of these products are the following.

Tamino XML Server is the web-enabled native database system of the Software AG [Tam03]. The approach of Tamino is to store the entire document without fragmenting and to concentrate on fast search algorithms (full-text and indexing). The Software AG does not release any details about the storage format. It certainly uses know-how from Adabas [Ada03] – the company's relational DBMS that also has hierarchical features (nested tables). Tamino is suitable for document-centric XML. Like in XIS, documents are seen in their entirety only, access to document parts is not provided. XML documents are put in collections, queries can be asked on collections as well as on single documents. Tamino contains an extension of XPath that allows fast searching and sorting methods.

An open-source product is Xindice, the native XML database of Apache's XML project [Xin03]. Its proprietary storage format is model-based. Documents are put in collections, like in Tamino. It is also possible to build collections of collections. XPath is used for searching across collections of documents. To search efficiently, indices can be created on elements and on attributes. Full-text search is not available. To save parts of documents, XUpdate can be used. Xindice is suitable for collections of many small documents.

Infonyte [Inf03a] is designed for storing single large documents up to one terabyte. To achieve this, a DOM implementation is used, that builds the object hierarchy not in main memory but in the background memory of the DBMS. It is therefore called "Persistent DOM". XQL, XPath and XSLT can be used for querying documents. Infonyte is a native XML DBMS.

As mentioned above, native XML databases are not appropriate for *RelAndXML*, since they save documents in their entirety instead of in fragments. Furthermore, the companies' discretion about technical details makes these products rather uninteresting for our research project.

3.2.4   Object-Relational Database Systems

Object-relational database management systems (ORDBMS) provide very robust database technology. An XML interface to a relational DBMS offers the combination of this technology and the advantages of XML delivery. Complex queries may be written in SQL and their results may be formatted as XML. The data may be accessed through all existing applications to an object-relational database, like query tools, browsers, data loaders, and data exporters. Other important aspects are the sophisticated transaction management and the recovery mechanisms in today's ORDBMSs. Moreover, the interoperability with other object-relational databases can be used for the federation of databases.

The most popular ORDBMSs (Oracle, IBM DB2) and the relational system Microsoft SQL Server are all XML enabled. There also exists numerous middleware, that is mostly DBMS-independent [Bou03b]. Middleware also works with systems which are not XML enabled (e.g. PostgreSQL). With XML add-ons, the data may be manipulated with XML query languages like XPath and XQuery. XML documents can be saved in their entirety, as larger or smaller fragments.

We think, the object-relational technology is the most interesting for our research project, because of its versatility, robustness, and the enormous standardization efforts for SQL (see Subsection 3.3.1). Also when we started this project back in 1999, the XML query languages were just about to be designed, so we thought it was safer to have SQL access at least.

The following section discusses object-relational technology in more detail. Object--relational data can be fairly easily expressed in XML, but loading data from an arbitrary XML document into an object-relational database can be difficult; we cover methods for storing XML documents in object-relational databases in Chapter 4.

3.3   Various Aspects of Object-Relational Database Management Systems

This section about various aspects of object-relational DBMSs starts with an overview of the SQL standard. Next, we describe some features like new data types and recursive SQL that we either are using for *RelAndXML* or at least considered using during the design phase (in this case, we explain why we decided against using them). The availability of these features influenced our decision for a particular DBMS. We also explain the standardization efforts for XML extensions (SQL/XML) and the quite different current XML extensions.

We considered four DBMS products and refer to the versions, which were the latest in March 2003. These are

- IBM DB2, Version 8.1   – called DB2   – homepage at [DB203]
- IBM Informix, Version 9.3.1   – called Informix   – homepage at [Inf03b]
- Oracle9i, Release 2   – called Oracle   – homepage at [Ora03]
- PostgreSQL, Version 7.3   – called PostgreSQL   – homepage at [Pos03]
- Microsoft SQL Server 2000   – called SQL Server   – homepage at [MSS03]

We have worked with DB2, PostgreSQL and SQL Server, but not with Oracle or Informix. The information, which features are implemented in which system, is mainly taken from [Tür03] or other cited literature, where we could not test the features ourselves. SQL Server actually is not advertised as being object-relational, although it has many of the newer features (but not the "object" features explained below). We therefore refrain from writing "(object-) relational systems" in the following.

3.3.1 SQL Standards

The SQL standard has undergone many revisions and its parts were often published in between versions. We give a short overview.

The first standard for SQL was passed by the American National Standards Institute (ANSI) in 1986 and was accepted by the International Organization Standardization (ISO) in 1987. The following work on the standard was called SQL2, and in 1992, a major revision called SQL-92 was passed by ANSI and ISO. We assume, the reader is familiar with this version of the standard and give just a brief refresher, which aspects are included: SQL-92 provides a *data definition language* (DDL) to create tables, a *data manipulation language* (DML) with constructs to insert, update, and delete rows from tables as well as *query expressions* to retrieve selected rows from one or more tables. It also has a set of basic data types for columns, a notion of privileges to control access to tables as well as declarative integrity constraints and the notion of referential integrity. Other features include outer joins, catalogues, domains, and temporary tables.

Accordingly, the work on the next generation was called SQL3; some parts of it were published in 1999 as SQL:1999[2]. Since SQL:1999 integrates aspects from object-oriented

---

[2]A note about the naming conventions: The change to use a colon instead of the hyphen was made to align with the conventions of the ISO, rather than with the ANSI's conventions as before. This reflects the increasingly international character of the SQL standards. The change to add the century indicator to the year was made in 1999, when the "Year 2000 problem" was addressed throughout the world. Nevertheless, the unofficial term SQL-99 is also in use.

technology, most DBMS products with SQL:1999 features call themselves *"object-re-lational"*. *Structured types* are user-defined types with attributes and methods, and are similar to classes. A class hierarchy can be built, since structured types can be subtyped. Objects of structured types do not necessarily have an object identifier such that a basic object-oriented aspect is not realized.

We are mainly interested in the new basic data types and type constructors (see Sub-section 3.3.2) and in recursive SQL queries (see Subsection 3.3.3 on page 48). Recursive queries are part of SQL/PSM (Persistent Stored Modules), which specifies the ability to define functions and procedures which are written in SQL or in a host programming lan-guage and which are invoked from SQL programs. These functions and procedures are commonly called *stored procedures*, because they are actually stored right in the database itself. SQL/PSM also defines a number of procedural SQL statements like WHILE-DO, REPEAT-UNTIL, IF-THEN-ELSE, and CASE, besides the recursive SQL queries, thus making SQL computationally complete for the first time.

The next revision of the SQL standard is expected to be published in 2003, thus called SQL:2003. It contains all parts of SQL:1999 as well as a new part called SQL/XML (XML-Related Specifications) that we describe in Subsection 3.3.5. Apart from SQL/XML, SQL:2003 only contains some miscellaneous new functionality like a data type for big in-tegers and a statement called MERGE which is a combined insert and update command. Generated columns, sequence generators and identity columns are covered in Subsec-tion 3.3.4.

The vendors still have considerable work to do to conform to SQL:1999 and cur-rently, no product is claiming conformance to SQL:1999. According to Melton and Si-mon ([MS02], p. 55), "conformance to Core SQL means that a DBMS product contains all of Entry SQL-92, plus much of Intermediate SQL-92 and some of Full SQL-92, plus a few new SQL:1999 features."[3] The authors describe SQL:1999 in two volumes thor-oughly [MS02, Mel03]. A more compact book which also covers SQL:2003 is [Tür03] by Türker. A comprehensive overview of the SQL standard is given in the article [MKF+03] by Michels et al.

3.3.2   SQL:1999 – New Basic Data Types and Type Constructors

SQL:1999 defines three new basic data types: BOOLEAN, BLOB, and CLOB.

The BOOLEAN data type can have one of three literal values: TRUE, FALSE, or UN-KNOWN; yet, UNKNOWN and NULL are considered the same[4]. This data type is imple-mented in Informix and PostgreSQL, but not in DB2, Oracle and SQL Server. The usual

---

[3]The authors provide a comprehensive list of the Core SQL features in [MS02], pages 801–807.

[4]We think this is more likely a source of confusion than an aid to the user.

work-around is to declare a CHARACTER(5) data type with permissible values of 'true' or 'false'.

The CLOB data type is used for "Character Large Objects" (for documents); the BLOB data type is meant for handling "Binary Large Objects", e.g. for embedding a GIF file within a database row. The size of CLOB and BLOB columns can be specified using K, M, or G for kilo-, mega-, or giga-, respectively. Both data types are supported by all the mentioned DBMS products. In PostgreSQL and SQL Server, the CLOB data type is called TEXT; the BLOB data type is called TYPEA in PostgreSQL and IMAGE in SQL Server.

SQL:1999 offers the anonymous type constructors ROW and ARRAY. The type constructor ROW allows to create *nested tables*: the value of a single column is a tuple of values, for example if an address column contains the fields street, city, and zipcode. It is only implemented in Informix. The ARRAY type, which is implemented in PostgreSQL, allows to store ordered collections of values in one column of a database table up to the specified maximum cardinality, for example, if a column knowledgeOfLanguages holds an array with up to eight languages. Informix has a LIST type which is not included in SQL:1999.

Structured types, which allow to store objects with attributes and methods, are implemented in DB2 and Oracle.

	SQL: 1999	DB2	Informix	Oracle	PostgreSQL	SQL Server
BOOLEAN	✔	✕	✔	✕	✔	✕
BLOB	✔	✔	✔	✔	TYPEA	IMAGE
CLOB	✔	✔	✔	✔	TEXT	TEXT
ROW	✔	✕	✔	✕	✕	✕
ARRAY	✔	✕	✕	✕	✔	✕
LIST	✕	✕	✔	✕	✕	✕
Structured Types	✔	✔	✕	✔	✕	✕
Recursive Queries	✔	✔	✕	✔	✕	✕

Table 3.1: SQL:1999 Features in ORDBMS Products

Table 3.1 summarizes the features and their availability in current ORDBMS products. In *RelAndXML*, we have boolean attributes, but they can almost as well be saved with a character data type, so this is not a necessary feature. We use the CLOB data type, which is fortunately available in all of these DBMS products. We explained the ROW, ARRAY and LIST type constructors, since they are used in a special clause of recursive SQL and/or in some papers that we cite in Chapter 4.

3.3.3 SQL:1999 – Recursive Queries

With recursive SQL queries, we are able to retrieve all the nodes which are connected to a specific node in a graph or we can compute the transitive closure of a set of nodes, for example. These questions might arise when XML documents are saved as a set of edges.[5] Recursive queries are realized with the help of named queries. A *named query* is a query expression, which can be referenced and therefore reused within the immediately following query. It is like a temporary view, which only exists during the execution of the recursive query.[6]

As an example, we save the source and target nodes of the edges of two XML graphs in an Edge table (see Table 3.2).

Edge	
source	**target**
A1	A2
A2	A3
A1	A4
A4	A5
A5	A6
A6	A7
B1	B2
B2	B3
B3	B2

Graph A   Graph B

Table 3.2: Edge table for two XML Graphs

First, we try to retrieve all the nodes that can be reached from the root "A1", called the *transitive closure* of "A1". The corresponding recursive query is shown as Listing 3.1 on the facing page. The WITH clause defines the named query Treedata with columns source and target as the result set of the two subqueries in parentheses which are combined with UNION ALL. The first subquery (lines 3 to 5) is called *initial subquery* or *seed* and finds a set of rows from which the recursion is started. Our seed consists of the first two rows

---

[5]See Section 4.2 on page 73.

[6]The advantage to a usual view is that a temporary view does not need to be deleted with a DROP VIEW command.

in the table shown as Table 3.3(a). The second subquery (lines 7 to 9) is the *recursive subquery*, which accumulates more rows based on their relationship with the rows in the seed; this is done with a join between Treedata and Edge. The recursion terminates when no new tuples are found; this is called a *fixpoint* (the problem of termination is addressed below). The last line contains the *non-recursive part* of the coded query; it retrieves all rows from the temporary view and thus returns the result set of our recursive query shown as Table 3.3(a).

Listing 3.1 Recursive query to retrieve the transitive closure of "A1"

```
1    WITH RECURSIVE Treedata(source, target) AS
2    (
3        SELECT source, target
4        FROM Edge
5        WHERE source = 'A1'
6    UNION ALL
7        SELECT In.source, Out.target
8        FROM Treedata In, Edge Out
9        WHERE In.target = Out.source
10   )
11   SELECT * FROM Treedata;
```

---

source	target
A1	A2
A1	A4
A1	A3
A1	A5
A1	A6
A1	A7

(a) Nodes connected to "A1"

source	target
A1	A2
A2	A3
A1	A4
A4	A5
A5	A6
A6	A7

(b) Edges of the graph A

Table 3.3: Result sets of the basic recursive queries

If we replace line 7 of our recursive query by

```
7            SELECT In.target, Out.target
```

we get all the edges of the graph A (see Table 3.3(b)).

The termination of recursive queries is a central problem. A recursive query is safe (always terminates) when it has a fixpoint. A fixpoint exists when the number of rows being accumulated into the result of a recursive query is monotone increasing. The monotonicity assures that no tuples of the temporary view are updated or deleted. It can be violated by negation with NOT EXISTS, EXCEPT, INTERSECT, and DISTINCT, as well as by aggregate and arithmetic functions. Therefore, these SQL features are only allowed in the non-recursive part at the end of a recursive query.

The termination is also put at risk when the data contains cycles like the XML graph B in Table 3.2. SQL:1999 provides two ways to deal with cycles: limit the depth of recursion or use a CYCLE clause. We give examples for both possibilities. The recursive query in Listing 3.2 retrieves all the edges of graph B and is limited to depth 4. The depth is computed in the third column, called connections, of the named query; it is initialized with 0 in the initial query and increased by 1 in each step of the recursive query.

Listing 3.2 Recursive query with depth limited to 4   ·

```
1    WITH RECURSIVE Treedata(source, target, connections) AS
2       (
3           SELECT source, target, 0
4           FROM Edge
5           WHERE source = 'B1'
6       UNION ALL
7           SELECT In.target, Out.target, In.connections+1
8           FROM Treedata In, Edge Out
9           WHERE In.target = Out.source
10          AND In.connections < 4
11      )
12   SELECT DISTINCT source, target FROM Treedata;
```

The temporary view Treedata of this recursive query contains duplicate rows (see Table 3.4(a)), since the recursion already occurs at depth 3. The duplicates are eliminated by the non-recursive part in line 12, giving us the result set shown as Table 3.4(b). The disadvantage of limiting the depth of recursion is that the limit must be chosen by the user who might not know the data well enough for this task.

source	target	connections
B1	B2	0
B2	B3	1
B3	B2	2
B2	B3	3
B3	B2	4

(a) Temporary view

source	target
B1	B2
B2	B3
B3	B2

(b) Result set

Table 3.4: Temporary view and result set for the depth-limited query

The second way to ensure termination of recursive queries is using a CYCLE clause. Listing 3.3 shows a version of Listing 3.2 with a CYCLE clause instead of the depth limit. The temporary view of this query is shown in Table 3.5 and its result set is the same as in Table 3.4(b); the explanation follows below.

Listing 3.3 Recursive query with cycle clause

```
 1   WITH RECURSIVE Treedata(source, target) AS
 2      (
 3          SELECT source, target
 4          FROM Edge
 5          WHERE source = 'B1'
 6      UNION ALL
 7          SELECT In.target, Out.target
 8          FROM Treedata In, Edge Out
 9          WHERE In.target = Out.source
10      )
11   CYCLE source, target SET cyclemark
12   TO '1' DEFAULT '0' USING cyclepath
13   SELECT DISTINCT source, target FROM Treedata;
```

The cycle detection of the DBMS saves the accumulated values of the source and target cells in column cyclepath, which needs as data type a combination of ARRAY and ROW. The cyclemark is set to its default value '0', as long as there are no duplicates in cyclepath. When a duplicate is found, cyclemark is set to '1', and the query execution is continued with the non-recursive part.[7]

---

[7]The values of cyclemark need not be '0' and '1', but they must be of type CHAR(1).

source	target	cyclemark	cyclepath
B1	B2	0	[(B1,B2)]
B2	B3	0	[(B1,B2),(B2,B3)]
B3	B2	0	[(B1,B2),(B2,B3),(B3,B2)]
B2	B3	1	[(B1,B2),(B2,B3),(B3,B2),(B2,B3)]

Table 3.5: Temporary view for the query with CYCLE clause

SQL:1999 also provides *recursive views*, which are views that are defined with a recursive query. In Listing 3.4, we show an example with a recursive view Data with all successor nodes of the node "A4" of graph A (see Table 3.2). The view is shown as Table 3.6.

Listing 3.4 Creating a view with a recursive query

```
1   CREATE RECURSIVE VIEW Data(source, target) AS
2   WITH RECURSIVE Treedata(source, target) AS
3   (
4       SELECT source, target FROM Edge WHERE source = 'A4'
5   UNION ALL
6       SELECT In.target, Out.target
7       FROM Treedata In, Edge Out
8       WHERE In.target = Out.source
9   )
10  SELECT * FROM Treedata;
```

---

source	target
A4	A5
A5	A6
A6	A7

Table 3.6: The view Data

Oracle and DB2 support recursive queries, but not the CYCLE clause[8]. Note that in DB2, the keyword RECURSIVE must be omitted. Informix, PostgreSQL, and SQL Server do not support recursive queries. For *RelAndXML*, we use recursive queries in the algorithm Rel2XML (see Section 7.4) that generates an XML document from the

---
[8]Oracle and DB2 do not support the ARRAY and ROW type constructors necessary for the CYCLE clause.

relational tables. We also implemented a version of this algorithm that works without recursive queries, such that we are not restricted to use a particular DBMS.

3.3.4   SQL:2003 – Generated Columns, Sequence Generators and Identity Columns

SQL:2003 defines three possibilities for generating or computing values of columns. Identity columns combine the concepts of generated columns and sequence generators.

A *generated column* is a column whose value is computed from values of other columns in the same row. To give an example, suppose we had an Employee table with columns salary and bonus. A column total_pay could be declared to be a generated column with the keywords GENERATED ALWAYS AS and the formula salary + bonus.

```
ALTER TABLE Employee
ADD COLUMN total_pay GENERATED ALWAYS AS (salary + bonus)
```

A *sequence generator* produces a sequence of numerical values. It has the following syntax; most of it is self-explanatory.

```
CREATE SEQUENCE <sequencename>
[START WITH <initialvalue>]
[INCREMENT BY <incrementalvalue>]
[NO MINVALUE | MINVALUE <minimalvalue>]
[NO MAXVALUE | MAXVALUE <maximalvalue>]
[NO CYCLE | CYCLE]
```

NEXT VALUE FOR <sequencename> returns the next value of a sequence.[9] When the maximal value is reached, and the option NO CYCLE is in use, the DBMS throws an exception. When CYCLE is in use, the generation starts again with the minimal value. Sequence generators can be used when identity columns are not implemented in the chosen DBMS.

When a column is declared to be an *identity column*, then the DBMS will generate a unique value for that column in each row as it is inserted into the table.

```
ALTER TABLE Employee
ADD COLUMN dbmsId INT GENERATED ALWAYS AS
    IDENTITY (START WITH 10000
    MINVALUE 10000 MAXVALUE 99999 NO CYCLE)
```

---

[9]nextval('<sequencename>') in PostgreSQL

Generated and identity columns are features that where implemented in DB2, and then integrated into SQL:2003. The implementations in PostgreSQL and SQL Server do not conform to this standard. Sequence generators are supported by all mentioned DBMS products except by SQL Server.

	SQL: 2003	DB2	Informix	Oracle	PostgreSQL	SQL Server
Generated Columns	✔	✔	✕	✕	✕	(✔)
Sequence Generators	✔	✔	✔	✔	✔	✕
Identity Columns	✔	✔	✕	✕	(✔)	(✔)

Table 3.7: SQL:2003 Features in ORDBMS Products

We considered using sequence generators or identity columns for the primary key columns in *RelAndXML*, but decided against it for the following three reasons. First, for *RelAndXML* we need identity values which are unique within the system and not just within the table.[10] Second, within the GUI we need an identity for a new object as soon as it is created and long before it is inserted into the database for the first time. Third, we want to send all the INSERT commands for an XML document at once; this is impossible with sequence generators since generated primary key values are usually used as foreign key values in other INSERT statements for the same document.

3.3.5   SQL:2003 – SQL/XML

SQL/XML will standardize the various, mostly incompatible XML extensions that OR-DBMS products have today (see the following Subsection 3.3.6). It consists of three major features: an XML data type, functions to generate XML from SQL data, and a mapping from SQL tables to XML documents.

Cells of the new XML data type are able to store XML documents, individual elements, sequences of elements (with no single root), text nodes, and mixed content. Attributes can exist within an element, but they are not legal XML values themselves. XML comments and processing instructions are not currently allowed within the XML data type.

The following functions produce values of the new XML data type from SQL data.

- XMLGEN generates an XML value based on a query that is written in XQuery.

---

[10]One can work around this by adding the tablename as prefix, everytime a value is read from the database and cutting it before writing to the database, but that solution is tedious.

- XMLELEMENT creates XML elements from database columns, these elements might also have attributes which are specified with XMLATTRIBUTES.

- XMLFOREST produces a sequence of XML elements from a sequence of columns.

- XMLCONCAT concatenates several XML elements.

- XMLAGG produces a single XML value from a group of XML values.

In the following example, we use XMLELEMENT to create an element for each specified row of an Assignment table. For more information and examples, see [EM02b, Mel03, SQL03, Tür03].

```
SELECT a.sid,
          XMLELEMENT(NAME "A", XMLATTRIBUTES(a.sid), a.number)
          AS "data"
FROM Assignment a
```

sid	number
1002	Assignment 2
1003	Assignment 3

(a) Table Assignment

sid	data
1002	<A sid="1002">Assignment 2</A>
1003	<A sid="1003">Assignment 3</A>

(b) Result Set

SQL/XML also defines a mapping from tables to XML documents, see Subsection 4.1.1 on page 60. The standardization has not been finished, so some features might still be changed or added.

3.3.6 XML Extensions of Some Current ORDBMS Products

The DBMS products DB2, Oracle and SQL Server do have an XML extension, but they all use proprietary storage formats and functions. The standard XML data type is very similar to the one used in Oracle. Informix and PostgreSQL do not have an XML extension. Hopefully, the vendors will implement SQL/XML soon.

When we were in the design phase for *RelAndXML*, the XML extensions were still in their infancy and had no standard. So we decided not to use any of these XML features, but to implement the shredding and generating of XML documents with Java and JDBC (see Chapter 7).

Nevertheless, we explain the XML concepts of DB2, Oracle and SQL Server shortly in the remainder of this subsection. For more information, see [KM03, Sch03b] or the web sites of the products [DB203, Ora03, MSS03].

IBM DB2

The IBM DB2 XML Extender gives a choice between storing the entire XML document or storing it as a collection of XML fragments, and therefore is a hybrid XML database. With the *XML Column* option, an entire XML document is saved as an XML user-defined type (UDT) column. Three UDTs are provided: XMLFile for a reference to an external XML file, XMLVarchar for short internal documents, and XMLCLOB for long internal documents. User-defined functions (UDFs) are used for insert, select and update operations. Elements and attributes can be indexed for faster search results. Document order is preserved and a DTD need not be available.

XML Collection denotes methods for an XML to object-relational tables mapping and vice versa. This is realised with a group of stored procedures with the prefix dxx like dxxGenXML for composing and dxxShredXML for decomposing XML. The mapping is described with a *Data Access Definition* (DAD), which is an XML document itself. It can access both XML Columns and SQL standard types. XML Collection only works well for valid XML, since a DAD conforms to a DTD. The document structure is preserved by the DAD, but the complete document order is lost.

The *TextExtender* adds full text functionality as known from information retrieval.

Oracle 9i

Oracle 9i provides the *Oracle XML Developer's Kit* (Oracle XDK) which includes methods to read, transform, manipulate, and generate XML documents. The *XML SQL Utility* (XSU) includes three essential components: the export of database content as XML documents, the native storage of XML with the data type XMLType with the possibility to use XPath queries, and the structured mapping of XML data in relations and attributes.

The export and import methods map object-relational structured types to the structure of an XML document: an attribute with a structured type is mapped to a nested subelement. Referential integrity constraints are mapped to ID/IDREF links within a document.

The data type XMLType, which is new in version 9i, saves XML documents or fragments; it is similar to the data type XML in SQL/XML. The storage is internally based on CLOBs. SELECT statements with embedded XPath expressions are used to search on these columns. There are no update operations on parts of a XMLType cell. To change the data it must be replaced in its entirety.

Oracle 9i supports the hybrid storage of XML documents. Data-centric parts can be saved in usual SQL data type columns and document-centric parts in XMLType columns. Queries and export methods work on all data types such that combined XML documents can be retrieved as well.

Information retrieval methods are also included in this DBMS.

Microsoft SQL Server 2000

The XML extension of the SQL Server is called SQLXML despite its limited similarity to the standard SQL/XML. The focus is on publishing relational data as XML. SQLXML extends SQL by adding a FOR XML clause to the end of the SELECT statement, which formats the rows of the result set as an XML document. Options to the FOR XML clause allow formatting the data in an attribute-oriented or element-oriented way.

XML documents can be stored with the aid of the function OpenXML, which reads an XML document and returns a result set according to an XPath expression. By using this result set in an INSERT command, the extracted data can be stored in the database.

Microsoft SQL Server does not have a special XML data type and provides only functionality for data-centric, but not for document-centric XML. It therefore is an XML enabled database.

3.4 Summary: RelAndXML as Middleware for an OR-DBMS

The aim of this chapter was to select the appropriate type of database for *RelAndXML*. We showed that native XML databases are not suitable because of their characteristic to save entire XML documents. XML enabled databases do not preserve comments and document order, so they cannot be used without an add-on. *RelAndXML* should be based on a hybrid XML database or be implemented as middleware, such that the special characteristics of hypertext-centric XML can be supported.

We described several data models and chose the object-relational because of its promising versatility. We considered the most popular (object-) relational DBMS products IBM DB2, IBM Informix, Oracle, PostgreSQL, and Microsoft SQL Server (see Table 3.8).

	SQL: 1999	DB2	Informix	Oracle	PostgreSQL	SQL Server
BOOLEAN	✔	✗	✔	✗	✔	✗
CLOB	✔	✔	✔	✔	TEXT	TEXT
Recursive Queries	✔	✔	✗	✔	✗	✗
XML Data Type	SQL: 2003	✗	✗	(XMLType)	✗	✗
XML Extension	✗	✔	✗	✔	✗	✔

Table 3.8: SQL Features in ORDBMS Products

Of the various SQL:1999 features, we need the CLOB data type for larger XML fragments, which is supported by all the mentioned products. The BOOLEAN data type is
a desirable feature for *RelAndXML*, but with no big consequences if it is not available.
We use recursive queries in the algorithm Rel2XML (see Section 7.4) that generates an
XML document from the relational tables. Since we also implemented a version of this
algorithm working without recursive queries, this feature does not need to be available,
but probably gives a speed bonus.

The new standard XML data type of SQL:2003 could of course be used instead of
CLOB, but it is not yet available in the mentioned products – the XMLType of Oracle is
closest to the standard. We refrained from using the proprietary XML extensions, since
they require an implementation that is very product-specific and would not work with
other products without considerable effort.

In summary we meet our goal to keep *RelAndXML* independent from a single particular DBMS product. Any of the mentioned products would be appropriate. Our decision
was also influenced by the need for free or at least inexpensive licences for the products.
We worked with a free trial version of DB2 to implement the recursive queries and then
decided to switch to the free PostgreSQL product.

Chapter 4

Storing XML Documents in Object-Relational Databases

Storing XML documents in databases has been a major topic in database research in the last few years [CFP00, Wid99]. Approaches to this topic are dependent on the desired application area and can be divided into two main directions: some concentrate on data-centric and others on document-centric documents. To name the basic possibilities: The XML data can be stored as one document, divided into smaller sections and stored as fragments, or broken up into individual elements. Document-centric documents are often stored in their entirety, whereas data-centric documents are often shredded into individual elements.

The concept for storing data-centric XML in (object-) relational database systems ((O)RDBMS) is to define a mapping between the DTD and the database schema [Bou01, RP02, STH$^+$99]. The advantages of these mappings are that query writing is easy and that the DBMS (or the XML Parser using the DTD) checks data consistency. The obvious draw-back is that these mappings only work for valid XML.

Many approaches for storing document-centric XML documents fragment down to every single element [FK99b, Kud01, SYU99], which leads to a large number of database tuples per document. This makes the reconstruction of documents expensive. These approaches do preserve document order, but they make reusing text modules impossible.

In this chapter, we start developing an approach to store hypertext-centric XML in an object-relational database. We plan to save the data-centric text modules in a *Core*, the document-centric additional text and metadata in an *Extension*, and the data-centric XSLT text modules as *Presentation*. The details of this approach will be explained in Chapter 5. Let us now take a look at both data-centric and document-centric approaches to find the best combination.

4.1   Some Methods to Save Data-Centric XML

In this section, we discuss different aspects of the storing of data-centric XML. In the first subsection, we describe how to present data from a relational database as an XML document, especially the representation of foreign key-modeled relationships. For *Rel-AndXML*, we will use the *object-based mapping with representation of associated objects* contained in this subsection. We describe in the second subsection how a DTD can be mapped to a database schema, such that valid XML documents can be stored in the database. Since there are many papers on this topic, we summarize the most important ones in the third subsection. In the last subsection, we explain briefly how to derive a DTD from a database schema.

4.1.1   Mapping Database Content to XML Documents

To explain the publishing of relational data as an XML document, we use a database consisting of the tables Assignment and Course, which are shown with some sample content in Table 4.1. Note that there is a many-to-one relationship between the tables through the foreign key columns courseUid and courseVersion in Assignment.

Assignment				
uid	**version**	**published**	**number**	**dateOfIssue**
A2	1.0	false	Assignment 2	October 14, 2002
A3	1.0	false	Assignment 3	October 21, 2002

deadline	**courseUid**	**courseVersion**
Monday, October 21, 2002, 4pm	FCS1	1.0
Monday, October 28, 2002, 4pm	FCS1	1.0

Course			
uid	**version**	**name**	**semester**
FCS1	1.0	Fundamentals of Computer Science 1	Winter 2002/03

Table 4.1: Tables Assignment and Course

Table-based mapping

The simplest mapping is the *table-based mapping*, which maps tables to an XML document in the following way: A root element is created with the name of the table. It contains a row element for each row in the table. Each row element consists of a sequence of column elements, each with the name of the column. Each column element contains a data value. This mapping is *element-oriented*, since it maps everything to an element. The content of the Assignment table leads to the following XML data:

```
<assignment>
    <row>
        <uid>A2</uid>
        <version>1.0</version>
        . . .
    </row>
    <row>
        <uid>A3</uid>
        <version>1.0</version>
        . . .
    </row>
</assignment>
```

When several tables are mapped, the root element is named like the database (here <infdb>) and contains the table elements (here <assignment> and <course>).

```
<infdb>
    <assignment>
        . . .
    </assignment>
    <course>
        . . .
    </course>
</infdb>
```

The table-based mapping is used by many of the middleware products that transfer data between an XML document and a relational database [Bou03a], and it is defined in SQL/XML [MKF+03].

A variation of this mapping uses the table name element instead of the row element and the plural of the table name instead of the table name element.

```
<assignments>
    <assignment>
        <uid>A2</uid>
        <version>1.0</version>
        . . .
    </assignment>
```

```
<assignment>
    <uid>A3</uid>
    <version>1.0</version>
    ...
</assignment>
</assignments>
```

Also, the mapping can specify XML attributes for some or all of the columns (in the latter case, it is called *attribute-oriented*); the following lines show a mixed mapping.

```
<assignment uid="A3" version="1.0" published="false"
            courseUid="FCS1" courseVersion="1.0">
    <number>Assignment 3</number>
    <dateOfIssue>October 21, 2002</dateOfIssue>
    <deadline>Monday, October 28, 2002, 4pm</deadline>
</assignment>
```

The table-based mapping is also suitable for result sets of queries. The rows of the result set are listed in one of the mentioned manners with a resultset element as root element.

There are two ways to deal with null values: (1) do not include the corresponding element or attribute to the document, or (2) include the corresponding element or attribute to the document with a zero-length string value.

At first sight, the first way seems to be the more correct way, since the common definition for a null value is to be "just not there" for unkown reasons, and a zero-length string value is clearly different from a null value. The second way is used to show what elements and attributes are available and not (yet) filled, and is therefore often used [Bou01]. We use this way for *RelAndXML*. The user works with a GUI and chooses from text modules, which suggest elements and attributes to the user. In this situation it is the best solution to give elements and attributes a zero-length string value as long as they are not yet filled.

Object-based Mapping with Representation of Associated Objects

So far, we can map complete tables or result sets. Now, we are interested in a mapping suitable for objects, for example to get an XML document with all the relevant information on "Assignment 3". For this mapping we want to improve the representation of associated objects – up to now, only the foreign key values are mapped. For example, the assignment above contains the foreign key values for the corresponding course, but not the course itself. Also, when the course is mapped in a table-based way, it does not have any information about its assignments. Therefore, we suggest to use elements for the relationships and to consider including the corresponding objects. Listing 4.1 shows an XML document for "Assignment 3" where the associated course element is included within an element isAssignmentOfCourse into the document. Note that this is exactly our running example "Assignment 3", see Listing 2.8 on page 24.

Listing 4.1 Copy of XML running example "Assignment 3"

```
<assignment uid="A3" version="1.0" published="false">
    <number>Assignment 3</number>
    <dateOfIssue>October 21, 2002</dateOfIssue>
    <deadline>Monday, October 28, 2002, 4pm</deadline>
    <isAssignmentOfCourse>
        <course uid="FCS1" version="1.0">
            <name>Fundamentals of Computer Science 1</name>
            <semester>Winter 2002/03</semester>
        </course>
    </isAssignmentOfCourse>
</assignment>
```

To prevent an infinite loop, we have to choose at most one side of the relationship, which includes the other side. It is okay to include all columns of the corresponding table, but not to consider other relationships. One might think that for one-to-many relationships it should always be the "one" side which includes the "many" side, because this fits naturally into the XML tree structure. We prefer to choose the side that makes semantically the most sense. For example, we need the information about the name and the semester of a course to be printed on each assignment, so we include the course (which is the "one" side of the relationship) into the assignment (which is the "many" side). When the XML document for the course is assembled, we get a list with its assignments (see Listing 4.2 on the next page), which is more useful than a huge document including all assignments completely.

In the literature, there often is no element for the relationship [STH+99, Bou01] or just one relationship element which includes all associated objects [SSB+01]. In the first case, the mapping does not work properly whenever there is more than one relationship between two tables. In the latter case, relationship attributes, e.g. ordinal, must be part of the associated element, e.g. assignment in Listing 4.2, which is semantically less clear.

Listing 4.2 XML running example "Course FCS 1"

```
<course uid="FCS1" version="1.0">
    <name>Fundamentals of Computer Science 1</name>
    <semester>Winter 2002/03</semester>
    <hasAssignments ordinal="2">
        <assignment uid="A2" version="1.0" published="false">
            <number>Assignment 2</number>
            <dateOfIssue>October 14, 2002</dateOfIssue>
            <deadline>Monday, October 21, 2002, 4pm</deadline>
        </assignment>
    </hasAssignments>
    <hasAssignments ordinal="3">
        <assignment uid="A3" version="1.0" published="false">
            <number>Assignment 3</number>
            <dateOfIssue>October 21, 2002</dateOfIssue>
            <deadline>Monday, October 28, 2002, 4pm</deadline>
        </assignment>
    </hasAssignments>
</course>
```

Also, the relationship names should be unique in order to support reflexive relationships as well.

We developed the *object-based mapping with representation of associated objects* for the *Core* part of *RelAndXML* and summarize it here. Examples are shown in Listing 4.1 and in Listing 4.2.

1. Each database tuple is mapped to an XML element with the name of the database table.

2. A subset of the database attributes is mapped to XML elements, the rest to XML attributes.

3. Relationships are mapped to relationship elements with unique names.

4. For each relationship, there is a rule fixing whether to insert the associated object.

4.1.2 Mapping a DTD to a Database Schema

The mappings of a DTD to a database schema describe rules for the creation of tables, columns, and foreign key relationships for the element and attribute types of the DTD. If *RelAndXML* is to be used for a new application area having a DTD, we can use such a mapping to define an appropriate *Core* database schema.

We follow the descriptions of Bourret, who offers a comprehensive version in [Bou01] and a summary in [Bou03a]. The *object-relational mapping*, as the author calls it, is used by all currently available XML-enabled relational databases and some middleware products. For this mapping, an *object view* is defined for an XML document that models the data in the document as a tree of objects similar to our graph presentation (see Subsection 2.1.7). The object view is then mapped to a database schema. *Complex element types* are element types which have attributes, contain subelements and/or mixed content. They are usually viewed as classes and mapped to a table. *Simple element types* have PCDATA-only content and are, as well as single-valued attributes, usually viewed as properties and mapped to columns.

We quote the five steps to generate a relational schema from a DTD from [Bou03a] and explain them using the *SmallCore* DTD from Chapter 2, which is shown again in Listing 4.3. The resulting table structure is shown in the Tables 4.2 to 4.5; a discussion follows afterwards.

Step 1: For each complex element type, create a table and a primary key column.

We have four complex element types giving us four tables. Assignment, Question, AsHasQu, and Paragraph get as primary key the column a_sid_pk, q_sid_pk, ahq_sid_pk, and p_sid_pk, respectively. See Table 4.2.

Step 2: For each element type with mixed content, create a separate table in which to store the PCDATA, linked to the parent table through the parent table's primary key.

The explanation for this step in [Bou03a] is not very concrete. We decided to create a table Paragraph_MixedContent, in which the mixed content of a paragraph is saved little by little. To store the sibling order, we add an ordinal column. The table structure and its content for "Assignment 2" are shown in the Tables 4.3 and 4.4. Note that the number of null values in this mixed content table grows with the number of alternative elements in the DTD. In the earlier paper [Bou01], the author suggests to create one table for the PCDATA and one for each alternative. This clearly requires more joins for the reconstruction of objects. The content of these tables for the running example

---

Listing 4.3 Copy of the *SmallCore* DTD

```
1    <!-- Filename: smallcore.dtd -->
2    <!ENTITY % basic "uid CDATA #REQUIRED
3                      version CDATA #REQUIRED
4                      published (false | true) 'false'
5                      date CDATA #IMPLIED">
6    <!ELEMENT assignment (number, dateOfIssue?, deadline?, asHasQu+)>
7    <!ATTLIST assignment %basic;>
8    <!ELEMENT asHasQu (question)>
9    <!ATTLIST asHasQu ordinal CDATA #IMPLIED>
10   <!ELEMENT question (paragraph)>
11   <!ATTLIST question %basic;
12                      marks CDATA #IMPLIED>
13   <!ELEMENT number (#PCDATA)>
14   <!ELEMENT dateOfIssue (#PCDATA)>
15   <!ELEMENT deadline (#PCDATA)>
16   <!ELEMENT paragraph (#PCDATA | emph)*>
17   <!ELEMENT emph (#PCDATA)>
```

"Assignment 2" (see Listing 2.7 on page 23) is shown in Table 4.5. We suggest to use stop tags for mixed content as explained on page 69.

Step 3: For each single-valued attribute of that element type, and for each singly-occurring simple child element, create a column in that table. If the child element type or attribute is optional, make the column nullable.

The single-valued attributes and singly-occurring simple child elements are mapped to the columns as shown in Table 4.2.

Step 4: For each multi-valued attribute and for each multiply-occurring simple child element, create a separate table to store values, linked to the parent table through the parent table's primary key.

This step does not apply to our example. Note that we could use an ARRAY column instead of the separate table if this type constructor is available in the chosen DBMS.[1]

Step 5: For each complex child element, link the parent element type's table to the child element type's table with the parent table's primary key.

---

[1] See Subsection 3.3.2 on page 46.

There are three primary key/foreign key references: AsHasQu gets a foreign key a_sid_fk to Assignment, Question gets a foreign key ahq_sid_fk to AsHasQu, and Paragraph is connected to Question by the foreign key q_sid_fk. See Table 4.2.

Table **Assignment**

Column name	Value is nullable	Column created in
a_sid_pk	no	Step 1
uid	no	Step 3
version	no	Step 3
published	no	Step 3
date	yes	Step 3
number	no	Step 3
dateOfIssue	yes	Step 3
deadline	yes	Step 3

Table **Question**

Column name	Value is nullable	Column created in
q_sid_pk	no	Step 1
uid	no	Step 3
version	no	Step 3
published	no	Step 3
date	yes	Step 3
marks	yes	Step 3
ahq_sid_fk	no	Step 5

Table **AsHasQu**

Column name	Value is nullable	Column created in
ahq_sid_pk	no	Step 1
ordinal	no	Step 3
a_sid_fk	no	Step 5

Table **Paragraph**

Column name	Value is nullable	Column created in
p_sid_pk	no	Step 1
q_sid_fk	no	Step 5

Table 4.2: Tables for the *SmallCore* DTD

Table **Paragraph_MixedContent**		
Column name	Value is nullable	Column created in
p_sid_fk	no	Step 2
pcdata	yes	Step 2
emph	yes	Step 2
ordinal	no	Step 2

Table 4.3: Paragraph_MixedContent table for the *SmallCore* DTD

Paragraph	
p_sid_pk	**q_sid_fk**
4001	2001[a]
4002	2002[b]

[a]2001 is the system generated identifier for the question with uid="Q2" and version="1.0"
[b]2002 is the system generated identifier for the question with uid="Q1" and version="1.0"

Paragraph_MixedContent			
p_sid_fk	**pcdata**	**emph**	**ordinal**
4001	Prove		1
4001		Lemma	2
4001	2.2.		3
4002	Prove		1
4002		Lemma	2
4002	2.1.		3

Table 4.4: Content of the Paragraph tables for "Assignment 2"

Paragraph_Emph		
p_sid_fk	**emph**	**ordinal**
4001	Lemma	2
4002	Lemma	2

Paragraph_PCDATA		
p_sid_fk	**pcdata**	**ordinal**
4001	Prove	1
4001	2.2.	3
4002	Prove	1
4002	2.1.	3

Table 4.5: Content of the Paragraph tables for "Assignment 2" as in [Bou01]

Discussion

Data Types   Since DTDs do not contain concrete data type information, the column data types and lengths must be specified by hand.[2] As mentioned before, we will use mostly character data types for the InfDB database except for the sibling-order saving columns ordinal, which are integers.

Null Values   XML supports the concept of null data through optional element types and attributes. If the value of an optional element type or attribute is null, it simply is not included in the document. Therefore, they are mapped to nullable columns.[3]

Primary Keys   The algorithm adds an additional primary key column to each table. If XML data is retrieved from the database without including the primary key into the XML document, it will not be possible to save an updated version of the document back to the database (since new primary key values would be generated). On the other hand, if the primary key is included, it should also be added to the DTD, otherwise the retrieved XML documents will not be valid any more. Another solution is to specify already existing attributes as primary key columns if possible. For example, the columns uid and version are a suitable primary key for the tables Assignment and Question.

Changing Names   Of course, names can be changed during the mapping. This is necessary, for example, if the XML names are SQL keywords like SELECT or ORDER (SQL is not case-sensitive), or contain characters that are not included in the character set of the DBMS, e.g. map the element Straße to the column Strasse.

Complexity of the Database Schema   In the example we have seen that we easily get a fair amount of tables. Reducing the number of tables is desirable, since it reduces the average number of joins needed for evaluating queries. Also, some tables might be sparsely populated like the mixed content tables.

To reduce the number of tables we could decide to use complex element types with mixed content as *stop tags*. This means the mixed content is saved as one piece including the comprised tags. Also, we could combine AsHasQu and Question to a single table; asHasQu is then a so-called *wrapper element*. This gives us two tables, shown in Table 4.6, instead of six tables as before. (To be exact, the combined AsHasQu-Question

---

[2]Note that data types and lengths can be predicted from an XML Schema document.

[3]As mentioned before, attributes containing zero length strings and empty elements are not null, but in spite of this definition, it is quite likely that XML documents will use empty (zero-length) strings to represent null values.

table should be named AsHasQu like its wrapper element, but we apply the above rule on changing names.) The new columns in Question are marked with "Step 6". Table 4.7 shows the content of the Question table for "Assignment 2". We use stop tags in the *Core* of *RelAndXML*. Approaches with stop tags are called *hybrid* [KM00].

Table **Assignment**		
Column name	Value is nullable	Column created in
a_sid_pk	no	Step 1
uid	no	Step 3
version	no	Step 3
published	no	Step 3
date	yes	Step 3
number	no	Step 3
dateOfIssue	yes	Step 3
deadline	yes	Step 3

Table **Question**		
Column name	Value is nullable	Column created in
q_sid_pk	no	Step 1
uid	no	Step 3
version	no	Step 3
published	no	Step 3
date	yes	Step 3
marks	yes	Step 3
paragraph	no	Step 6
ordinal	no	Step 6
a_sid_fk	no	Step 6

Table 4.6: Reduced tables for the *SmallCore* DTD

Question				
q_sid_pk	uid	version	published	marks
2001	Q2	1.0	false	null
2002	Q1	1.0	false	null

paragraph	ordinal	a_sid_fk
Prove <emph>Lemma</emph> 2.2.	2	1002[a]
Prove <emph>Lemma</emph> 2.1.	1	1002

[a]1002 is the system generated identifier for "Assignment 2".

Table 4.7: Question table for "Assignment 2"

Quality of the Database Schema   The greatest mismatch between database tables and a DTD is for many-to-many relationships, because the notion of many-to-many does not really exist in DTDs. Suppose we update the DTD with the following lines

```
<!ELEMENT question (paragraph, isQuestionOf*)>
<!ELEMENT isQuestionOf (assignment)>
```

to represent that not only an assignment can have multiple questions, but that a question might be present on several assignments also. (Remember that a DTD does not specify the root element of the documents.) Note that now we have a *recursion* in the DTD. Bourret's algorithm would result in two one-to-many relationships instead of the many-to-many relationship; this must be fixed by hand. For papers concerned with finding recursion on DTDs, see the next subsection.

4.1.3 Related Work

Several researchers have published algorithms for the mapping of a DTD to a database schema; we describe and cite some of them next.

When the structure of the DTD is very complex, it can be reasonable to apply a number of rules to simplify the DTD first, in order to get a better database schema. Shanmugasundaram et al. provide such a set of rules in [STH+99]. Of course, XML documents valid to the original DTD can be stored in the database, but the sibling order is lost in some cases. To give an example, the rules simplify the element a specified as
<!ELEMENT a ((b|c|d)?,(d?|(e?,(b,b))*)*)>, where b, c, d and e are other elements, to
<!ELEMENT a (b*, c?, d*, e*)>.

The authors also introduce the notion of a *DTD graph*, which represents the structure of a DTD; its nodes are elements, attributes and operators in the DTD. A DTD graph is used to find recursion in the DTD. This is necessary since as many elements as possible are *inlined* into their parent element (in other words, the algorithm looks for suitable wrapper elements), but even in the case of a recursive DTD the inlining must come to an end.

The authors propose in [STH+99] three strategies to map DTDs into relational schemas and identify the *Hybrid Inlining algorithm* as being superior to the others in most cases.

Runapongsa and Patel present in [RP02] an improved version of the Hybrid Inlining algorithm and call it the *XORator algorithm*.

In [KM00], Klettke and Meyer present an algorithm that finds an object-relational hybrid mapping based on the DTD and statistics. The statistics are derived from sample XML document sets and some knowledge about queries on the XML document collection. The algorithm is based on the idea to find stop tags, which are called document fragments here, and to map them on database columns of type XML or CLOB (as available). Without explaining all the details, the results of the statistical calculations can be summarized as follows: Document fragments are built from elements which are often null, seldomly requested in queries and to whom's attributes and child elements the same criteria applies. Also, they suggest to use the ROW and LIST type constructors (only available in Informix, see Subsection 3.3.2 on page 46) for wrapper elements, which give a clearer database structure.

In [KC02], Kudrass and Conrad use structured data types and nested tables for an Oracle-specific mapping. Like the use of ROW and LIST, this approach makes the reuse of text modules impossible.

Bohannon et al. introduce in [BFRS02] a cost-based XML storage mapping engine similar to [KM00], which automatically finds the best mapping for a given configuration of an XML Schema, XML data statistics, and an XQuery workload.

The first hybrid approach was, to our best knowledge, published (but not explicitly using the term "hybrid approach") by Deutsch, Fernandez, and Suciu in the paper "Storing Semistructured Data with STORED" [DFS99]. Since there is no DTD available for the semistructured data, the authors use text-mining methods to identify structured document fragments that occur frequently within a sample document collection. Then, tables are defined to store the elements and attributes of these document fragments. Parts of the semistructured data that do not fit into the schema are stored in *overflow graphs*. The authors suggested a "semistructured data object repository" for the overflow graphs, when they wrote the paper in 1999. A column of the new XML data type would be a good choice as soon as available.

4.1.4   Deriving a DTD from a Database Schema

None of the Database-to-XML mappings presented in Subsection 4.1.1 needs a DTD, but we could derive one from the database schema, if desired. A short algorithm for generating a DTD from a relational schema is given in [Bou03a]; we quote it here without giving an example. This algorithm creates the relationships on both sides, but it does not use relationship names.

In order to generate a DTD from a relational schema, follow these steps:

- For each table, create an element type.
- For each data (non-key) column in that table, as well as for the primary key column(s), add an attribute to the element type or a PCDATA-only child element to its content model.
- For each table to which the primary key is exported, add a child element to the content model and process the table recursively.
- For each foreign key, add a child element to the content model and process the foreign key table recursively.

4.2 Some Methods to Save Document-Centric XML

Methods for document-centric XML work without any knowledge about the schema of the XML documents. As discussed in Chapter 3, native XML databases store the entire XML documents and concentrate on fast full text search algorithms. We are looking for an approach for the *Extension* of *RelAndXML*, where those parts of the document are saved that do not fit the *Core*: additional elements and attributes, comments, and processing instructions. We first concentrate on how to store additional elements. This section also shows why a *Core* is useful, rather than saving the complete document in the *Extension* part.

Highest priority first, we are especially interested in the following features:

1. For the reconstruction of a document, the number of databases accesses is as small as possible.
2. Reusing text modules without saving them twice.
3. Typical queries need few joins.
4. Inserting and deleting is easy.

Florescu and Kossmann discuss in [FK99b] (more verbose in the technical report [FK99a]) several basic approaches. All of them save the edges of a tree representation of an XML document, which is why they are called *edge approaches*. The authors tested the performance of the approaches and also suggested indexes for the database tables. Since attributes are treated like subelements, the exact reconstruction is not possible. Comments, processing instructions, and so on are not considered. We give a summary of their suggestions in the Subsections 4.2.1 to 4.2.4 and use "Question 4" of Listing 2.9 on page 24 as example – it is shown as XML tree in Figure 4.1 with attributes represented as subelements. Subsection 4.2.5 describes a path approach, where paths instead of single edges are saved, and gives reasons why we drop this approach.

4.2.1 Edge Approach

The *Edge* approach suggests to save all the edges of the XML tree in a single Edge table and the values in the leaves in separate value tables. The Edge table saves the parent node (source) and child node (target) of each edge together with its label (name), its ordinal number and a flag. The flag identifies an edge as internal reference (to an inner node of the XML tree) or as reference to a leaf with a value. The primary key is {source, ordinal}. The edges of the running example "Question 4" with the identifier "Q4" result in the tuples shown in Table 4.8.

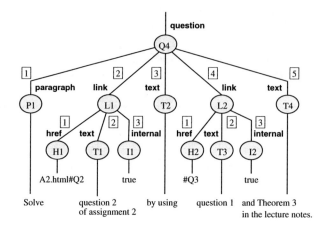

Figure 4.1: XML tree for "Question 4" with attributes represented as subelements

source	ordinal	name	flag	target
Q4	1	paragraph	string	P1
Q4	2	link	ref	L1
Q4	3	text	string	T2
Q4	4	link	ref	L2
Q4	5	text	string	T4
L1	1	href	string	H1
L1	2	text	string	T1
L1	3	internal	string	I1
L2	1	href	string	H2
L2	2	text	string	T3
L2	3	internal	string	I2

Table 4.8: Edge table for "Question 4"

Florescu and Kossmann [FK99b, FK99a] suggest two indexes for this table. The index on column source accelerates the reconstruction of objects when the object identifier is given (forward traversal). The index on {name, target} speeds up queries like "Find links with href='#Q3' " (backward traversal).

There is a separate *value table* for each data type, with the column sid as primary key and a value column. The flag column in the Edge table denotes the appropriate value table. Since "Question 4" contains strings only, there is a single ValueString table, shown as Table 4.9.

sid	value
P1	Solve
T2	by using
T4	and Theorem 3 in the lecture notes.
H1	A2.html#Q2
T1	question 2 of assignment 2
I1	true
H2	#Q3
T3	question 1
I2	true

Table 4.9: ValueString table for "Question 4"

4.2.2 Edge+Inlining Approach

The second approach *inlines* the values from the value tables into the Edge table which is then called EdgeInline table. One column per data type is added and the flag column is dropped. The inlining is done by a join on the target column in Edge with the sid column of the value tables. Apart from the two indexes that the Edge table has, the EdgeInline table gets an index on each of the new value columns. Supposing there were integer as well as string values, the EdgeInline table saves "Question 4" like shown in Table 4.10.

4.2.3 Binary Approach and Binary+Inlining Approach

The *Binary* approach suggests to put all edges with the same label in one table. This is a horizontal partitioning of the Edge table, using name as the partitioning attribute. Analogously, the *BinaryInline* tables are a horizontal partition of the EdgeInline table. Indexes on the source column, on the target column, and on each value column are suggested.

source	ordinal	name	target	valstring	valint
Q4	1	paragraph	P1	Solve	null
Q4	2	link	L1	null	null
Q4	3	text	T2	by using	null
Q4	4	link	L2	null	null
Q4	5	text	T4	and Theorem 3...	null
L1	1	href	H1	A2.html#Q2	null
L1	2	text	T1	question 2 of...	null
L1	3	internal	I1	true	null
L2	1	href	H2	#Q3	null
L2	2	text	T3	question 1	null
L2	3	internal	I2	true	null

Table 4.10: EdgeInline table for "Question 4"

For "Question 4", the partitioning results in five tables shown in Table 4.11 on the facing page.

The problem with this approach is that a new table has to be created whenever a new edge label is found. In a running system, this is possible but rather unpopular.

4.2.4   Comparing the Edge and Binary (with Inlining) Approaches

To compare the Edge and Binary approaches (with Inlining, resp.), we look at the aspects reconstruction, database size, query performance, ease of deleting and inserting objects, as well as reusing objects.

Reconstruction   To judge the efficiency of reconstruction we examine the cost of SQL statements necessary to reconstruct an object given its oid only, and including its children but excluding its further descendants. For the Edge approach, there is one indexed query to the Edge table needed with a join to each value table. For the Binary approach, an indexed query to *each* Binary table is needed, since it is unknown in which of them the subelements are included. The queries can be coupled with UNION. Afterwards, values are read from the value tables. When EdgeInline or BinaryInline are used, the joins to the value tables are left out. With each approach, the child elements can be ordered using the clause "ORDER BY ordinal". As can be seen clearly, the EdgeInline approach is most efficient for the reconstruction of flat objects and even more for the reconstruction of documents.

BinaryInline_Paragraph				
source	ordinal	target	valstring	valint
Q4	1	P1	Solve	null

BinaryInline_Link				
source	ordinal	target	valstring	valint
Q4	2	L1	null	null
Q4	4	L2	null	null

BinaryInline_Text				
source	ordinal	target	valstring	valint
Q4	3	T2	by using	null
Q4	5	T4	and Theorem 3...	null
L1	2	T1	question 2 of...	null
L2	3	T3	question 1	null

BinaryInline_Href				
source	ordinal	target	valstring	valint
L1	1	H1	A2.html#Q2	null
L2	1	H2	#Q3	null

BinaryInline_Internal				
source	ordinal	target	valstring	valint
L1	3	I1	true	null
L2	3	I2	true	null

Table 4.11: BinaryInline tables for "Question 4"

Database Size   With the Edge approach, the edge labels are saved redundantly in the name column resulting in a database larger than the database obtained when using the Binary approach. Inlining the values results in a smaller database, since the column oid is left out and the null values in the EdgeInline or BinaryInline tables need little space. So the BinaryInline approach gives the smallest database.

Queries   Queries are executed faster when using the Binary approach than the Edge approach, since joins with the large Edge table are expensive. Inlining accelerates queries because there are no joins to any value tables. So again, BinaryInline wins this aspect.

Inserting and Deleting Objects   Inserting an object into the Edge table and corresponding value tables or into the EdgeInline table is very easy, but may require updating the ordinal attribute of some sibling objects. Inserting an object into the Binary or BinaryInline tables causes difficulties if the edge label to this object is new, which means that a new table for this label has to be created. When these approaches are used for non-valid XML, it is very likely for new labels to show up at run time of the system. Although it is possible to create tables at run time (e.g. via JDBC) it is very unusual and most database administrators would not like this approach for safety reasons.

Deleting objects is easy in all approaches. The Binary and BinaryInline approaches might give some empty tables at run time, but this does not cause any problems.

Reusing Objects   Reusing objects is possible with all approaches. To insert "Question 4" into an "Assignment 4711", for example, there are just two new edges (asHasQu and question) necessary.

Since we find it unacceptable to create tables at run time, we decided to use neither the Binary nor the BinaryInline approach. From our point of view, where efficient reconstruction is most important, the EdgeInline approach wins this comparison. Nevertheless, we see the performance problems that a huge EdgeInline table causes. We also think that there should be tables for attributes and comments, and that the Edge approach with more sophisticated value tables can outstand the disadvantage of needing more joins. To see how we combine the EdgeInline and Edge approaches with these ideas, read Chapter 5.

Kudrass describes in [Kud01] an approach where the document identifier and the depth of the nodes are saved for each edge. Since this makes inserting, deleting, and reusing objects harder, we do not consider this approach.

4.2.5   Path Approach

Path approaches follow the idea to save paths from the root of the document to each node, instead of single edges like in the previous edge approaches. A path approach is given in [SYU99][4] – in the following we will describe a similar approach.

Since a path expression generally occurs several times in a document (especially in a document collection) there is a separate PathExpression table with columns pathID, which is a counter, and pathExp containing the path expression. Attributes get a preceding "@" to distinguish them from subelements. For the running example "Question 4", this gives the tuples shown in Table 4.12.

pathID	pathExp
1	/question/paragraph
2	/question/link/href
3	/question/link/text
4	/question/link/@internal
5	/question/text

Table 4.12: PathExpression table for "Question 4"

To preserve document order, the authors in [SYU99] use a text-oriented approach to number the elements. The numbering for "Question 4" is shown with numbers printed in bold type in Listing 4.4.

First, every single word of the text content gets an integer as number. Each start tag of an element gets a real number. Its integer part indicates the integer number of the preceding word and its decimal part indicates the position of the tag between the preceding and the succeeding word. This numbering approach does not reflect the tree structure at all.

Therefore, we use the following ordinal numbers instead: The ordinal number of a node of depth m in the tree has m stages. Each stage counts the nodes of this depth in the tree; the root always has the ordinal number 0. So in Figure 4.2 the five nodes of depth 1 get the ordinals 0.1, 0.2, 0.3, 0.4, and 0.5. Attributes do not need to have their own numbers, since they are identified by the ordinal of the corresponding element and their pathID.

In [SYU99] the authors suggest three tables for elements, attributes, and text. Since we have already seen the advantages of inlining the text values, we propose an "ElementIn-line" table. Remembering that "Question 4" belongs to an assignment with identifier

---

[4]A more verbose description of this approach which includes query translation from restricted XPath expressions to SQL can be found in [YASU01].

Listing 4.4 XML running example "Question 4" with ordinal numbers as proposed in [SYU99]

```
1     <question uid="Q4">(0.1)
2         <paragraph>(0.2) Solve(1)</paragraph>
3         <link internal="true">(1.1)
4             <href>(1.2) A2.html#Q2(2)</href>
5             <text>(2.1) question(3) 2(4) of(5) assignment(6) 2(7)</text>
6         </link>
7         <text>(7.1) by(8) using(9)</text>
8         <link internal="true">(9.1)
9             <href>(9.2) #Q3(10)</href>
10            <text>(10.1) question(11) 1(12)</text>
11        </link>
12        <text>(12.1)
13            and(13) Theorem(14) 3(15) in(16) the(17) lecture(18) notes.(19)
14        </text>
15    </question>
```

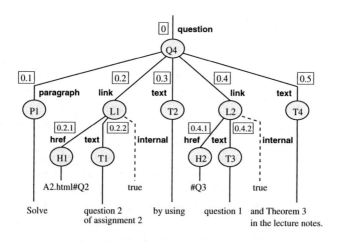

Figure 4.2: XML tree for "Question 4"

ElementInline			
docID	**pathID**	**ordinal**	**value**
A4	1	0.1	Solve
A4	2	0.2.1	A2.html#Q2
A4	3	0.2.2	question 2 of assignment 2
A4	5	0.3	by using
A4	2	0.4.1	#Q3
A4	3	0.4.2	question 1
A4	5	0.5	and Theorem 3 in the lecture notes.

Attribute			
docID	**pathID**	**ordinal**	**value**
A4	4	0.2	true
A4	4	0.4	true

Table 4.13: Element and attribute tables for "Question 4"

"A4", the corresponding tables look like shown in Table 4.13. Note that a docID is saved for each element.

Reconstruction   The reconstruction of an object, given its docID, path expression, and ordinal, needs two queries to ElementInline and Attribute each with a join to the Path table. Because of the join, the cost is slightly higher than with the EdgeInline approach. To reconstruct a document given its identifier, there are just two queries without any joins needed to retrieve all elements and all attributes, respectively. The path expressions can then be interpreted in main memory to reconstruct the XML tree. The number of queries for a reconstruction is smaller than for any of the edge approaches.

Database Size   The storage space needed by this approach is comparable to that of the BinaryInline approach since the path expressions are saved in a separate table.

Queries   Like for the Edge and EdgeInline approach, joins with the large ElementInline table are expensive.

Inserting and Deleting Objects   Inserting or deleting an object is costly, since the ordinals not just of the siblings but of all nodes further right and/or down in the tree have to be updated.

Reusing Objects   Since a document identifier is saved with each object, the reuse of objects in other documents is not possible in an intuitive way. One could try and save some kind of links from the new document to the reused objects in the old document, but this is likely to cause confusion when the old document is updated.

Path approaches are suitable to save documents in their entirety, but only when update operations do not occur frequently. Parts of documents cannot be reused in other documents. For these reasons, path approaches are not suitable for *RelAndXML* and are not considered any further in this thesis.

4.3 Conclusion: RelAndXML's Method to Save Hypertext-Centric XML

For *RelAndXML*, we combine a *Core* schema for the data-centric text modules of the XML document with an *Extension* schema for the document-centric parts, and a *Presentation* for the data-centric XSLT text modules (see Figure 4.3). There is also a *Metadata* part with structural information on the other parts used in the shredding and generating algorithms.

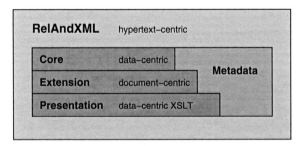

Figure 4.3: *RelAndXML* with *Core*, *Extension*, *Presentation*, and *Metadata*

The *Core* of *RelAndXML* is application-specific. We will use a *Core* for academic course material called *InfDB* (for Informatics Database). The data is transferred to XML according to the object-based mapping with representation of associated objects. The stored XML does not have to be valid, since the *Core* contains stop tags for saving mixed content and additional child elements.

Further additional elements, attributes, comments, and processing instructions are stored in the *Extension*. This part has an EdgeInline table for additional single elements, an Edge table, and some value tables for additional text modules, plus tables for attributes, comments, and processing instructions.

The data-centric XSLT text modules are stored in the *Presentation*, which also includes many stop tags.

Core and *InfDB*, *Extension*, *Presentation* as well as *Metadata* are explained in detail in the following Chapter 5.

Chapter 5

The InfDB Database Schema

In this chapter, we explain the full database schema of the *InfDB* database for academic course material as a result of the considerations in the previous chapters. Only the *Core* and a part of the *Extension* of the *InfDB* are application-specific. We modeled that area within the usual process of conceptual database design, of course taking into account knowledge about data-centric XML. The rest of the *Extension* as well as the *Presentation* and *Metadata* parts are independent of a specific application area. Whereas *Extension* and *Presentation* are designed based on knowledge from Chapter 4, the *Metadata* is designed to give information on the relational structure of the *Core*, *Extension*, and *Presentation*.

We use UML class diagrams as the graphical notation for conceptual database design. They comprise all the constructs of the extended Entity-Relationship model (EER model) with the advantage of being space-saving. Nevertheless, we write "entity type" for class and "entity" for object.

At the heart of the database model is the abstract entity type *Node* with a system generated identifier sid, a user identifier uid, a version number, and the attribute published (see Figure 5.1). *Node* is the supertype of the abstract entity types *CoreNode* and *ExtensionNode*, thus it connects the *Core* with the *Extension*. It also builds the connection to the *Presentation* as will be shown later.

Since *Node* is the supertype of all entity types in the *Core* and the *Extension*, there exists a key that is unique within these database parts. This was one reason for choosing a system generated identifier, the other reason is, that we want to be independent of a particular DBMS, but the database generated identifiers are quite diverse in different DBMSs as described in Subsection 3.3.4.

The remainder of this chapter includes a section for each of the *Core*, *Extension*, *Presentation* and the *Metadata* schema.

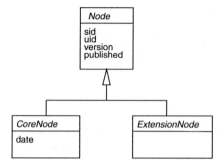

Figure 5.1: UML class diagram for the *InfDB* database – Overview

5.1 Core Schema

5.1.1 ER Schema for the Core

Within the *Core* schema, which is shown in Figure 5.2 on the next page, the entity type *CoreNode* is the supertype of all the other entity types. It inherits from its supertype *Node* the attributes sid, user identifier uid, version and published. The user identifier is a string chosen by the user, e.g. "DB1_Su02_A1" for the first assignment in the course "Databases 1" in the summer semester 2002. This way, it is easier for the user to find objects within the database. It is possible to save several versions of an object with the same uid. Objects that have been published should not be changed anymore, except for when the version number is increased. *CoreNode* also has an attribute date to save the last changes date.

The entity type Person saves the firstname, the lastname, the initials, and the academic title of a person. The entity types Assignment, Examination, Question, Part, and Figure have a N:1 relationship to Person to save the author, Course has this relationship to store the lecturer.

A Course is described by its name and semester. The entity type Assignment has a number, a date of issue and a deadline. An assignment belongs to a course, whereas a course comprises several assignments. Assignment and Question have a M:N relationship AsHasQues with the attribute ordinal that stores the order of the questions within an assignment. A Question has a single paragraph and the marks students can achieve. Some questions are building up on others, this is mapped with the recursive relationship QuesUsesQues. A Question might have several Parts that also have a single paragraph and some marks. A Part is semantically dependent of a question, therefore there must be at least one associated Question. This M:N relationship, called QuesHasPart, also saves

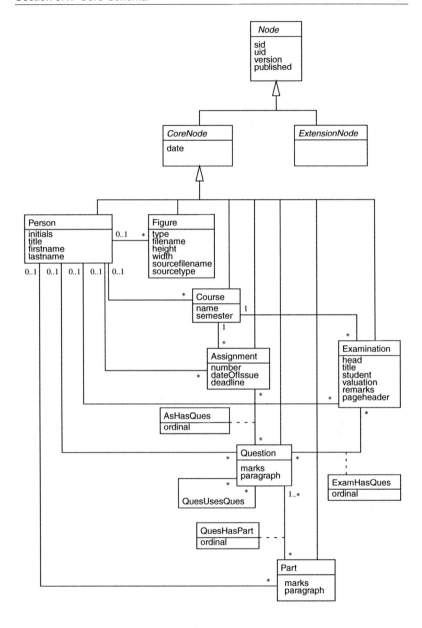

Figure 5.2: UML class diagram for the *InfDB* database – *Core*

the order of the parts with the attribute ordinal.

An Examination has a title, a head paragraph, some lines to write information about the student, about the valuation, some remarks and a pageheader. Like an Assignment, it has a N:1 relationship to Course and a M:N association with Question. The latter is called ExamHasQues and has an ordinal attribute.

A Figure has the attributes height, width, type, and filename. The attributes sourcetype and sourcefilename keep information if the figure was created using a graphics tool and then exported to have a suitable data format. Figures are not saved within the database, but on a file server.

5.1.2   Relational Schema for the Core

For the transfer of the EER schema into a relational schema, we use the well-known standard algorithm (see e.g. [EN00]). The relations are shown in Figure 5.3 on the facing page with underlined primary keys and foreign keys marked with a small arrow ↗; we give some explanations in the following.

Since *Node* and *CoreNode* are abstract entity types, there are no tables for them, but they transmit their attributes to their subtypes. Therefore the tables Course, Person, Assignment, Examination, Question, Part, and Figure each get the attributes sid, uid, version, published, and date.

Within the *Core*, the relations Course, Person, Assignment, Examination, Question, Part, and Figure get uid and version as primary key attribute and sid as secondary key. Why not choose sid as primary key, since it makes sure that every relationship within the *Core* needs just one foreign key attribute? The exchange of the *Core* should be as easy as possible. Suppose we want to use as *Core* an existent database. Then we add to each table the column sid. If *RelAndXML* was only able to cope with sid as primary key, we would have to add foreign key columns for every relationship in the database. We would also have to fill those columns with the correct values. If it is not a toy database, this cannot be done manually, so we would need a tool to accomplish this task. Also, if the database is still used by some other software, the change of the relationships is not appropriate. Therefore the foreign key relationships in the *Core* do not use the sid-columns. They are only used for the relationships in the *Extension* (see Section 5.2 on page 90).

Because of the 1:N relationships between Person and Course, Assignment, Examination, Question, Part, and Figure respectively, those relations get foreign key attributes (lecturerUID and lecturerVersion or authorUID and authorVersion) to Person. Assignment and Examination get foreign keys (courseUID and courseVersion) to the associated Course.

Course	{ sid, <u>uid</u>, <u>version</u>, published, date, name, semester, lecturerUid↗,
	lecturerVersion↗}
Person	{ sid, <u>uid</u>, <u>version</u>, published, date, initials, title, firstname, lastname}
Assignment	{ sid, <u>uid</u>, <u>version</u>, published, date, authorUID↗, authorVersion↗,
	number, dateOfIssue, deadline, courseUID↗, courseVersion↗}
Examination	{ sid, <u>uid</u>, <u>version</u>, published, date, authorUID↗, authorVersion↗,
	head, title, student, valuation, remarks, pageheader,
	courseUID↗, courseVersion↗}
Question	{ sid, <u>uid</u>, <u>version</u>, published, date, authorUID↗, authorVersion↗,
	marks, paragraph}
Part	{ sid, <u>uid</u>, <u>version</u>, published, date, authorUID↗, authorVersion↗,
	marks, paragraph}
Figure	{ sid, <u>uid</u>, <u>version</u>, published, date, authorUID↗, authorVersion↗,
	type, filename, sourcetype, sourcefilename, width, height}
AsHasQues	{ sid, <u>asUid↗</u>, <u>asVersion↗</u>, <u>quUid↗</u>, <u>quVersion↗</u>, ordinal}
ExamHasQues	{ sid, <u>emUid↗</u>, <u>emVersion↗</u>, <u>quUid↗</u>, <u>quVersion↗</u>, ordinal}
QuesHasPart	{ sid, <u>quUid↗</u>, <u>quVersion↗</u>, <u>paUid↗</u>, <u>paVersion↗</u>, ordinal}
QuesUsesQues	{ sid, <u>quUid↗</u>, <u>quVersion↗</u>, <u>usedUid↗</u>,<u>usedVersion↗</u>}

Figure 5.3: Relations of the *Core* Schema

There are four relations for the M:N relationships: AsHasQues, ExamHasQues, QuesHasPart, and QuesUsesQues with foreign keys to the associated relations. The foreign key attributes form the primary key of these relations. We add a secondary key sid for consistency reasons.

To create the tables, we have to choose data types for all of the columns. We use the CHAR or VARCHAR data types of different length for most columns. The CLOB data type is used for stop tag columns, when the character data is expected to be long, for instance the paragraph column in Question. We use INTEGER for the ordinal columns to ensure correct numerical ordering when the ORDER BY clause is used in queries. The CREATE commands for the *Core* are shown in the appendix in Section A.1 on page 157.

5.1.3 Running Example Tuples for the Core

Table 5.1 shows the *Core* tuples for the running example "Assignment 1" of Listing 2.6 on page 20. We omit the foreign key columns to Person and Course which have null values in this example. The paragraph of a Question is defined as a stop tag column.

Assignment				
sid	**uid**	**version**	**published**	**date**
assignment-1	DB1_Su2002_A1	1.0	true	06/14/02

number	**dateOfIssue**	**deadline**
Assignment 1	June 17, 2002	Monday, June 24, 2002, 4pm

AsHasQues			
sid	**asUid**	**asVersion**	**quUid**
asHasQues-2	DB1_Su2002_A1	1.0	DB1_Su2002_A1_Q1

quVersion	**ordinal**
1.0	2

Question				
sid	**uid**	**version**	**published**	**date**
question-3	DB1_Su2002_A1_Q1	1.0	true	06/07/02

marks	**paragraph**
4	Translate the Company ER schema into a relational schema.

Table 5.1: Tables in the *Core* schema

5.2   Extension Schema

5.2.1   ER Schema for the Extension

For the *Extension* schema we extend the Edge and Edge+Inlining approaches from Florescu and Kossmann [FK99b] described in Subsections 4.2.1 and 4.2.2. Before going into details, we give a short overview: We use Edge and EdgeInline entity types similar to the ones in [FK99b] and add the entity types EdgeAttribute, EdgeComment, EdgeProcInstr to support attributes, comments, and processing instructions, respectively.   All of these entity types are called *Edge entity types*. Instead of the simple value tables / entity types from [FK99b], we use *ExtensionNode entity types* that save complete text modules.

We now explain the *Extension* schema, which is shown in Figure 5.4, in detail:

The *ExtensionNode entity types* are subtypes of the abstract entity type *ExtensionNode* and store structured text modules that unlike the entity types in the *Core* schema do not have fixed relationships to other entity types. Compared to [FK99b], they are extended value entity types that work together with the Edge entity type. They are application-specific and in *InfDB*, we have the two entity types Link and Keyword. The entity type Link has the attributes date, the target href, text and internal. If internal is true, the link connects to another object or document within the system; otherwise it is an external link to any web page. The entity type Keyword has the attribute name. As mentioned in Subsection 4.2.4, the disadvantage of the Edge approach compared to the EdgeInline approach is that we need additional joins to the value tables. The *ExtensionNode entity types* overcome this disadvantage by compressing several XML pieces into one database tuple.

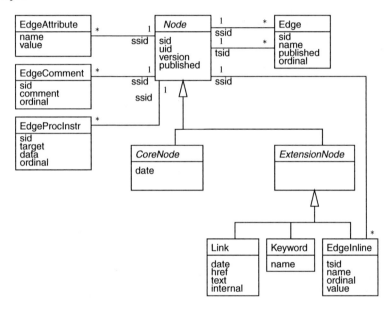

Figure 5.4: UML class diagram for the *InfDB* database – *Extension*

The rest of the entity types in the *Extension* schema are called *Edge entity types* and save the edges to *ExtensionNodes* as well as all still remaining XML fragments. The edges between *ExtensionNodes* are saved with the Edge entity type. As in [FK99b] it has the attributes name and ordinal. Through the mandatory N:1 relationships to *Node*, it gets the attributes ssid and tsid, which are equivalent to source and target in [FK99b]. We add the attributes sid and published for consistency reasons. We drop the flag attribute from [FK99b], since Edge is only used for connections to *ExtensionNodes*.

The EdgeInline entity saves all the still left-over XML elements. It saves an edge together with information about a node and therefore is, exactly speaking, an *Edge* as well as an *ExtensionNode* entity type. As a subtype of *ExtensionNode*, it inherits the attributes sid, uid, version, and published. The inherited attribute sid is renamed to tsid, since it is the identifier of the stored target node. The entity type also needs an associated source *Node* (ssid). Furthermore, it has the attributes sid (for consistency reasons), name, ordinal and value. Taking the renaming of source to ssid, target to tsid, and valstring to value into account, our EdgeInline table is the same as in [FK99b] with additional columns sid, uid, version, and published.

Attributes are saved with the entity EdgeAttribute. They have a name and a value and belong to a *Node*. This means especially, that any XML element of the *Core* or the *Extension* can have additional XML attributes. A *Node* may also contain comments and processing instructions. Comments are saved in EdgeComment with the attributes sid, comment, and ordinal. Processing Instructions are saved in EdgeProcInstr with the attributes sid, target, data, and ordinal.

The reason why Edge, EdgeInline, EdgeComment, and EdgeProcInstr each have a system identifier sid is to ease the implementation: Otherwise the combination of the foreign key ssid and ordinal would be the primary key of the table. But ordinal is an attribute that often changes its value such that it is not appropriate to be used as part of a primary key. Without sid we would have modeled Edge as recursive M:N relationship to *Node*, and EdgeComment and EdgeProcInstr as weak entity types.

We thought about adding an entity type EdgeDocType with the attribute doctype to save an internal or external DTD. This entity type would have an association to *Node*. Initially, we wanted to add this feature to provide HTML entities like α for α in *RelAndXML*. But if entities are defined, elements have to be declared as well. The XML parser does not accept entity declarations on their own, which means that it prints an error message for each element, for instance:

```
Element "assignment" must be declared.
```

Since *RelAndXML* is not designed for data-centric, valid XML, it is not very useful to provide a feature that forces documents to be valid. Furthermore, every Unicode character can be saved in *RelAndXML* directly, the problem is to provide a way of inserting it directly into the document (there is no α on the keyboard). We tried "Copy & Paste" from other programs such as the browser view of Netscape and that works well. It is also possible to wrap the values of EdgeInline with CDATA sections. In this way, HTML entities can be used in EdgeInline elements, since CDATA sections are ignored by the XML parser.

5.2.2 Relational Schema for the Extension

The relational schema for the *Extension*, which is shown in Figure 5.5, has five application-independent relations for *Edge* entity types and two application-specific *ExtensionNode* relations.

Edge	{ <u>sid</u>, ssid↗, tsid↗, ordinal, name, published}
EdgeInline	{ <u>sid</u>, ssid↗, tsid, ordinal, name, value, uid, version, published}
EdgeAttribute	{ <u>ssid</u>↗, <u>name</u>, value}
EdgeComment	{ <u>sid</u>, ssid↗, comment, ordinal}
EdgeProcInstr	{ <u>sid</u>, ssid↗, target, data, ordinal}
Link	{ <u>sid</u>, uid, version, published, date, href, text, internal}
Keyword	{ <u>sid</u>, uid, version, published, name}

Figure 5.5: Relations of the *Extension* Schema

The table Edge receives two foreign keys ssid and tsid to the source and the target node respectively. The table EdgeInline also gets a foreign key ssid to the source node. Since EdgeInline combines an edge and a node, it also inherits the attribute sid from *Node*. It is renamed tsid, since it is the target node of the saved edge. The tables EdgeAttribute, EdgeComment and EdgeProcInstr each get a foreign key called ssid to the corresponding *Node*.

The CREATE commands for the *Extension* are shown in the appendix in Section A.2 on page 162. We use the CHAR, VARCHAR or CLOB data types for all of the columns except for the ordinal columns, which are INTEGER columns. The foreign keys cannot be realized with a foreign key constraint, since *Node* is an abstract entity type. We ensure data consistency within the *RelAndXML* system.

Although we do not use {ssid, ordinal} as primary key for the *Edge* tables as proposed in [FK99b], we create an index on these columns in the tables Edge, EdgeInline, EdgeComment, and EdgeProcInstr. Furthermore, we create an index on {name, tsid} in the tables Edge and EdgeInline as well as on value in EdgeInline as proposed in [FK99b]. In Link and Keyword, there is a secondary key on {uid, version}.

5.2.3 Running Example Tuples for the Extension

Table 5.2 on the following page shows the Extension tuples for the running example "Assignment 1". For its XML tree, please refer to Figure 2.2 on page 19 and for the XML source, see Listing 2.6 on page 20.

Edge				
sid	**ssid**	**tsid**	**ordinal**	**name**
edge-5	question-3	keyword-4	2	keyword

Keyword				
sid	**uid**	**version**	**published**	**name**
keyword-4	ERSchema	1.0	true	ER Schema

EdgeInline								
sid	**ssid**	**tsid**	**uid**	**version**	**published**	**ordinal**	**name**	**value**
edgeinline-7	assignment-1	exam-6	DB1-Exam-Su2002	1.0	true	4	exam	
edgeinline-9	exam-6	text-8	text-8	1.0	true	1	text	The exam is an
edgeinline-11	exam-6	strong-10	strong-10	1.0	true	2	strong	open book
edgeinline-13	exam-6	text-12	text-12	1.0	true	3	text	exam.

EdgeAttribute		
ssid	**name**	**value**
assignment-1	folder	DB1_Su2002

EdgeComment			
sid	**ssid**	**ordinal**	**comment**
edgecomment-14	assignment-1	3	Add a question about 3NF here.

Table 5.2: Tables in the *Extension* schema

5.3 Presentation Schema

5.3.1 ER Schema for the Presentation

With the *Presentation* schema we save the XSLT stylesheets which are applied to the XML documents to receive complete, ready-to-publish documents. Since XSLT stylesheets are valid XML documents we could take their DTD, derive a corresponding schema with the mapping described in Subsection 4.1.2 on page 65 and save the stylesheets analogous to the *Core*. But there is no advantage of storing stylesheets in such a fine-grained manner. As we have shown in Section 2.2, an XSLT stylesheet consists of an xsl:stylesheet or xsl:transform root element, an xsl:output element and a number of template rules. Other XSLT elements are usually contained within a template rule. We therefore use a coarse-grained manner to save stylesheets, which views them as a sequence of flat text modules rather than as an XML tree. Figure 5.6 on the next page shows the ER schema for the *Presentation*.

Xsl_Stylesheet saves the start and end sections of XSL stylesheets in its attributes starttags and endtags. The remainder of the attributes are an aid for the user but not included in the XSLT document: sid, uid, version, published, date, and description. Xsl_Template saves the XSL template rules in its attribute component. We add attributes for the XML attributes of xsl:template (match, name, priority, mode) to ease the search for template rules. Furthermore, it has the same helpful attributes as Xsl_Stylesheet: sid, uid, version, published, date, and description. Xsl_Stylesheet and Xsl_Template each have a N:1 relationship to the *Core* entity type Person to save the author. For this reason, the *Core* and the *Presentation* are NOT completely independent. However, when the *Core* is exchanged such that it has no Person entity type, we just leave these attributes empty.

Xsl_Stylesheet and Xsl_Template are related to each other by a many-to-many association. It has no ordinal attribute, since the order of the template rules within a stylesheet is not relevant. A general stylesheet should include default template rules for all of the *CoreNode* and *ExtensionNode* types. It can also contain more specific template rules. For instance, there is a special template rule for "Question 4" (see Listing 2.16 on page 35) in addition to the default rule for question. With Xsl_Node_Style, nodes or group of nodes and stylesheets can be connected. A group of nodes is specified by the node-name, e.g. "question". A sid column makes this design possible. The same applies to Xsl_Node_Template. Especially nodes saved in the EdgeInline table need their own template rules and it is useful to save the association in Xsl_Node_Template.

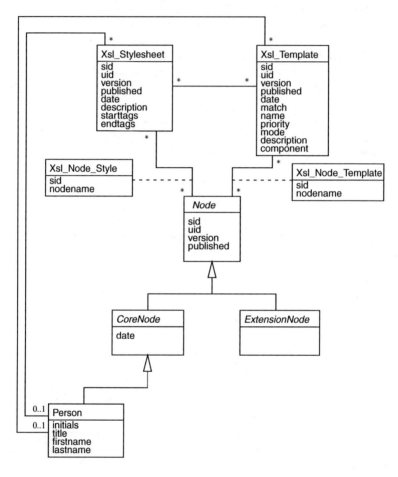

Figure 5.6: UML class diagram for the *InfDB* database – *Presentation*

5.3.2 Relational Schema for the Presentation

The relational schema for the *Presentation* is shown in Figure 5.7. Xsl_Stylesheet and Xsl_Template each have uid and version as primary key attributes, sid as secondary key, and get foreign key attributes to Person. The M:N relationship table between Xsl_Stylesheet and Xsl_Template is called Xsl_Style_Template. The relations Xsl_Node_Style and Xsl_Node_Template get foreign key attributes nuid, nversion to the associated *Node* as well as suid and sversion or tuid and tversion to the corresponding Xsl_Stylesheet or Xsl_Template. The primary key is sid, since nuid and nversion might be null when node-name has a not null value.

Xsl_Stylesheet	{ sid, <u>uid</u>, <u>version</u>, published, date, authorUid↗,
	authorVersion↗, description, starttags, endtags}
Xsl_Template	{ sid, <u>uid</u>, <u>version</u>, published, date, authorUid↗,
	authorVersion↗, match, mode, priority, name, description,
	component}
Xsl_Style_Template	{ <u>suid</u>↗, <u>sversion</u>↗, <u>tuid</u>↗, <u>tversion</u>↗}
Xsl_Node_Style	{ <u>sid</u>, nuid↗, nversion↗, nodename, suid↗, sversion↗}
Xsl_Node_Template	{ <u>sid</u>, nuid↗, nversion↗, nodename, tuid↗, tversion↗}

Figure 5.7: Relations of the *Presentation* Schema

For the CREATE commands for the *Presentation*, see Section A.3 on page 165 in the appendix. We use the CHAR, VARCHAR or CLOB data types for all of the columns. In Xsl_Node_Style and Xsl_Node_Template, the foreign key built out of nuid and nversion cannot be realized with a foreign key constraint, since *Node* is an abstract entity type. Instead, *RelAndXML* ensures the consistency of the data.

5.3.3 Running Example Tuples for the Presentation

We show some tuples for the running example stylesheet, which is shown as Listing 2.11 on page 32, in Table 5.3 on the following page.

Xsl_Stylesheet				
sid	**uid**	**version**	**published**	**date**
xsl_stylesheet-15	Stylesheet_HTML	1.0	true	06/14/02

description	**starttags**		**endtags**
null	<xsl:stylesheet ...>	<xsl:output .../>	</xsl:stylesheet>

Xsl_Style_Template			
sUid	**sVersion**	**tUid**	**tVersion**
Stylesheet_HTML	1.0	Templ_Assignment	1.0
Stylesheet_HTML	1.0	Templ_Question	1.0

Xsl_Template				
sid	**uid**	**version**	**published**	**date**
xsl_template-16	Templ_Assignment	1.0	true	06/14/02
xsl_template-17	Templ_Question	1.0	true	06/14/02

match	**mode**	**name**	**priority**
assignment	null	null	null
question	null	null	null

description	**component**
null	<xsl:template match="assignment">...</xsl:template>
null	<xsl:template match="question">...</xsl:template>

Table 5.3: Tables in the *Presentation* schema

5.4 Metadata Schema

Metadata is needed for the composing and fragmenting of XML documents according to the *Core* and *Extension* schema. The metadata is kept in the database as well, in the *Metadata* schema.

5.4.1 ER Schema for the Metadata

The ER schema for the *Metadata* is shown in Figure 5.8. To distinguish the entity types of this schema from the rest of the database, their names have the prefix RaxMeta (for *RelAndXML* Meta). The tables of the *Core*, *Extension*, and *Presentation* schemas are called *DB tables* in this section.

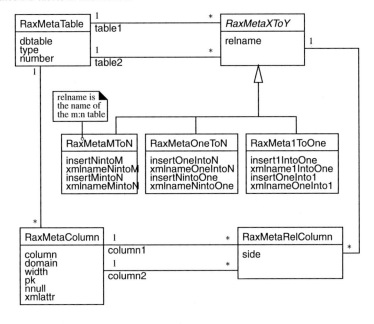

Figure 5.8: UML class diagram for the *Metadata* schema of the *InfDB* database

The entity type RaxMetaTable saves all DB tables (dbtable), their type ("core", "extension", "edge", "mn", "xsl", or "xslmn") and a number. The number orders the DB tables, when SQL statements must be executed in a certain order such that the foreign key constraints are not violated; for instance, an INSERT into Question must be executed before the INSERT into the M:N table AsHasQues.

The entity type RaxMetaColumn comprises information about all the columns of the DB tables and therefore has a N:1 relationship to RaxMetaTable. It saves the column name, the domain and the width of the table. The further attributes are booleans indicating if it is a primary key column (pk), if it is a not-null column (nnull) and if it should be shown as an XML attribute or as an XML element (xmlattr).

The remaining entity types save information about the relationships between the DB tables. There is an entity type for 1:1 relationships RaxMeta1ToOne, one for 1:N relationships RaxMetaOneToN, and one for M:N relationships RaxMetaMToN. They are subtypes of the abstract entity type *RaxMetaXToY*, which has the attribute relname for the name of the relationship and two N:1 relationships to RaxMetaTable qualifying the two related tables (table1, table2). For M:N relationships the relname must be the name of the M:N relationship table. The three subtypes have four attributes each, which are needed for (de-)composing documents, two for each side of the relationship:

> If insertXintoY is `true`, insert the X-side element with its attributes into the Y-side element and follow all of its associations as well. Else insert the X-side element with its attributes, but do not follow its associations. Use xmlname-XintoY to name the XML element for the relationship.

One might have used just the entity type RaxMetaXToY directly, with attributes relname, insertXintoY, xmlnameXintoY, insertYintoX, xmlnameYintoX, and an additional attribute type with values "1:1", "1:N" or "M:N" instead. That design is more compact, whereas the chosen design has more clarity.

To prevent the algorithm that composes XML documents (Rel2XML, see Section 7.4) from infinite loops, the *insertion graph* representing the insert rules must be cycle free. Its nodes are the entity types of the *Core*. There is an edge from entity type X to entity type Y if insertXintoY is true. The insertion graph for the *Core* of the *InfDB* is shown in Figure 5.9.

Since a foreign key relationship can have more than one column, the information about the foreign keys is put into a separate entity type RaxMetaRelColumn. This entity type has as attribute the side of the relation ("M", "N", "One" or "1"). Through a N:1 relationship with *RaxMetaXToY* the relationship name is known. Two relationships to RaxMetaColumn with the role names column1 and column2 give information about the related columns.

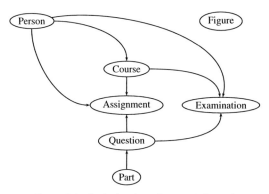

Figure 5.9: Cycle free insertion graph for *InfDB*

5.4.2   Relational Schema for the Metadata

The ER schema for the metadata results in the relations shown in Figure 5.10.

RaxMetaTable	{ <u>dbtable</u>, type, number}
RaxMetaColumn	{ <u>tablecolumn</u>, dbtable↗, column, pk, nnull, xmlattr, domain, width}
RaxMetaMToN	{ <u>relname</u>, table1↗, table2↗, insertNintoM, xmlnameNintoM, insertMintoN, xmlnameMintoN}
RaxMetaOneToN	{ <u>relname</u>, table1↗, table2↗, insertOneIntoN, xmlnameOneIntoN, insertNIntoOne, xmlnameNIntoOne}
RaxMeta1ToOne	{ <u>relname</u>, table1↗, table2↗, insert1IntoOne, xmlname1IntoOne, insertOneInto1,xmlnameOneInto1}
RaxMetaRelColumn	{ <u>relname</u>↗, <u>column1</u>↗, <u>column2</u>↗, side}

Figure 5.10: Relations of the *Metadata* Schema

The table RaxMetaColumn receives a foreign key dbtable to RaxMetaTable. It also gets an additional column tablecolumn, which is the primary key, containing the table-name and the columnname separated by a dot. This redundant information reduces the number of foreign key columns in RaxMetaRelColumn from four to two. So RaxMeta-RelColumn includes the associated columns (column1 and column2) and the name of the relationship relname; that combination is the primary key.

The tables RaxMeta1ToOne, RaxMetaOneToN, and RaxMetaMToN each get two foreign keys table1 and table2 to hold the relationship with RaxMetaTable.

The CREATE commands for the *Metadata* are shown in the appendix in Section A.4 on page 167. We use the CHAR or VARCHAR data types for most of the columns except for the number in RaxMetaTable and the width in RaxMetaColumn, which are INTEGER columns.

5.4.3   Running Example Tuples for the Metadata

Table 5.4 shows some tuples of the RaxMeta tables, especially for the M:N relationship between Assignment and Question.

RaxMetaTable		
dbtable	**type**	**number**
assignment	core	1
question	core	2
ashasques	mn	8
edgeinline	edge	14

RaxMetaColumn				
tablecolumn	**dbtable**	**column**	**pk**	**nnull**
assignment.sid	assignment	sid	false	true
assignment.number	assignment	number	false	false
question.paragraph	question	paragraph	false	false
ashasques.ordinal	ashasques	ordinal	false	true

xmlattr	**domain**	**width**
true	varchar	40
false	varchar	120
false	text	65535
true	int	4

RaxMetaMToN			
relname	**table1**	**table2**	**insertNintoM**
ashasques	assignment	question	true

xmlnameNintoM	**insertMintoN**	**xmlnameMintoN**
asHasQues	false	isQuestionOfAssignment

RaxMetaRelColumn			
relname	**column1**	**column2**	**side**
ashasques	assignment.uid	ashasques.asUid	m
ashasques	assignment.version	ashasques.asVersion	m
ashasques	question.uid	ashasques.quUid	n
ashasques	question.version	ashasques.quVersion	n

Table 5.4: Tables in the *Metadata* schema

5.5   Summary: Database Schemas for RelAndXML

A database schema for *RelAndXML* always consists of the following four parts: the *Core* and the *Extension* for XML documents, the *Presentation* for XSL documents, and the *Metadata* for metadata describing the other three parts.

The *Core* schema is an application-specific schema for data-centric text modules. In the *InfDB* database, the *Core* is designed for academic course material. The *Extension* has two parts: the *ExtensionNode* part and the *Edge* part. The *ExtensionNode* part is also application-specific; it contains tables for text modules which do not have fixed relations to other text modules but might appear everywhere in a document. The *Presentation* schema saves XSL documents and is application-independent. The *Metadata* schema saves information about the tables and foreign key relationships of the *Core*, *Extension*, and *Metadata*. The CREATE commands for the *InfDB* database are shown in Appendix A.

To use *RelAndXML* with another *Core* than the one in *InfDB*, we have to populate the *Metadata* tables with the according information. The administration tool of *RelAnd-XML* (see Chapter 6) generates INSERT commands for the tables RaxMetaTable and RaxMetaColumn that must be completed by hand: the user has to set the type and number in RaxMetaTable, the pk, nnull, and xmlattr values in RaxMetaColumn, and all the information about the relationships.

Outlook   We could extend the *Core* with tables for assignment solutions.

Chapter 6

Tutorial: How to use RelAndXML

In this chapter, we give a tutorial showing how to use the system *RelAndXML*.

The main window *XMLTree-Editor* offers seven tabbed panes to the user (see Figure 6.1): *DOM View* and *XML Source* to work with XML documents, *XSL Stylesheet*, *XSL Templates* and *XSL Source* to work with XSL documents, and *HTML Source* and *HTML View* to look at the resulting HTML documents.

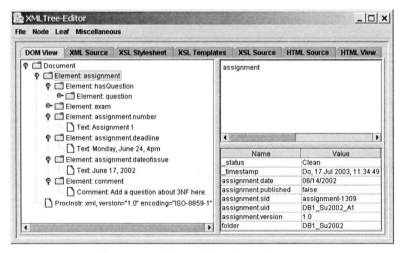

Figure 6.1: XMLTree-Editor with Assignment 1

The *XMLTree-Editor* has the four menus *File*, *Node*, *Leaf*, and *Miscellaneous*: *File* has menu items to create new XML or XSL documents, to open XML or XSL documents from the database, to save those documents to the database or to the file system, and to save the output HTML documents to the file system. The menus *Node* and *Leaf* are used for the *DOM View* only: *Node* lets the user insert or delete nodes to or from the DOM tree and *Leaf* allows to update the text or change the attributes of leaf nodes. The menu *Miscellaneous* lets the user open the *Administration* window and the *About* (the program) window.

In the following sections of this chapter, we explain the work with XML and XSL documents, as well as the viewing of HTML documents. After explaining various features, we give a conclusion and an outlook.

6.1   Working with XML Documents

When the system is started, it first displays the login dialog shown in Figure 6.2.

Figure 6.2: Login Dialog

We start with creating a new assignment in the *DOM View* pane by choosing the according menu item in the *File* menu (see Figure 6.3). A dialog opens where we insert the basic information about an assignment (see Figure 6.4). When we close this dialog with the OK button, a DOM view of this XML document is created (see Figure 6.5). The left frame, called *Tree*, shows a tree representation of the XML document. The upper right frame, called *Content*, shows the element names or the content of text nodes. In the lower right frame, called *Attributes*, the attributes of the selected node are shown. The selected element Assignment has, as the other elements also, an internal attribute _status="New" stating that the elements have not been inserted to the database.

Now, we choose *Save XML to DB* in the *File* menu, and then switch to the *XML Source view* (see Figure 6.6), which displays the serialized XML document in read-only mode. Note that the attribute _status now has the value "Clean" after the save operation.

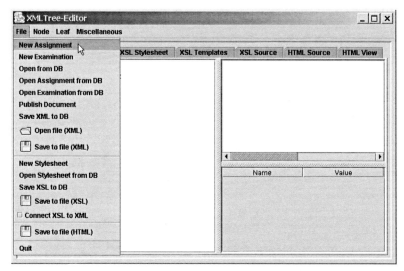

Figure 6.3: Menu - New Assignment

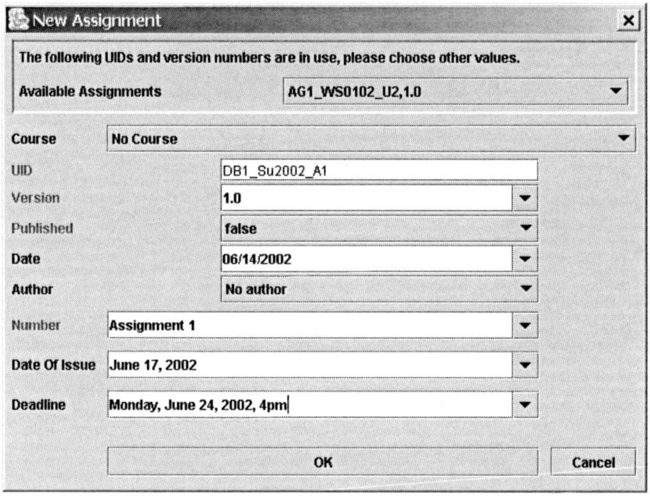

Figure 6.4: New Assignment Dialog

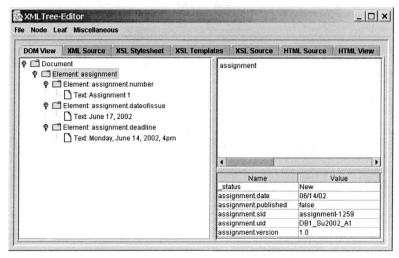

Figure 6.5: DOM View pane of Assignment 1

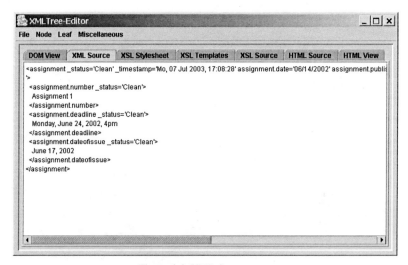

Figure 6.6: XML Source pane

The *DOM View* offers several windows, which we can open via the *Node* menu or context sensitive menus in the *Tree*, for inserting objects according to the *Core* and *Extension* tables - either new objects or loaded from the database. Figure 6.7 shows the context sensitive menu that shows up with a right click on the element assignment. We choose *Insert as Child - DB Question*, which will insert the new document fragment as the last child node. *Insert as Sibling* would insert the new document fragment as sibling node *before* the selected node (which is not possible here, since the selected node is the root element). With these two possiblities, we can control the order of the documents parts.

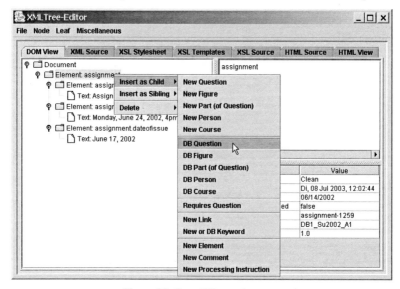

Figure 6.7: Open DB question menu

Figure 6.8 shows the dialog that helps the user to find a question. On the top, the user assembles an SQL statement to select questions. The combobox at the top offers for instance "SELECT * FROM question" to retrieve all questions. In the example shown, we ask for all questions with a keyword starting with 'ER'. After clicking of the *Find* button, we can flip through the selected questions in the lower part of the dialog. When we have found the right question, we press the *Insert* button. In Figure 6.9, we see the inserted question.

Only the windows for adding new or existing text modules according to the *Core* schema and the *ExtensionNode* tables Link and Keyword are specific to the student assignments application. All other parts of the implemented system can still be used if the

Core schema is replaced.

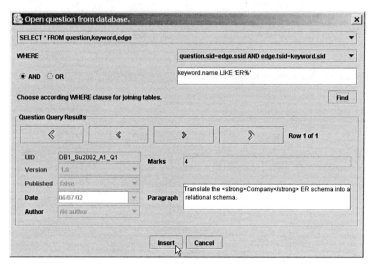

Figure 6.8: Open DB question dialog

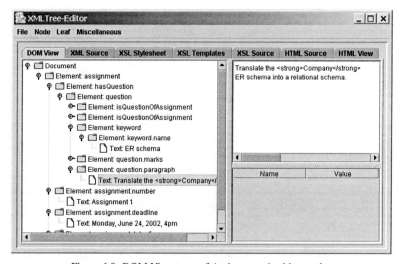

Figure 6.9: DOM View pane of Assignment 1 with question

Now we want to add the exam element, which is not part of the *Core*. We click the menu item *Insert as Child - New Element* and fill in the dialog shown in Figure 6.10. To the exam node we add a text element in the same way. To change the text content, we use the *Content* text panel and right-click there to choose *Update Text* as shown in Figure 6.11. (We could also choose the menu item *Leaf - Update Text*.) If we need single quotation marks in our text, we use ', since in SQL, strings are delimited by single quotation marks.

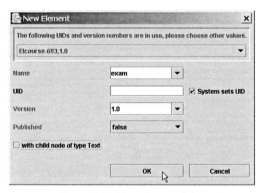

Figure 6.10: New element dialog

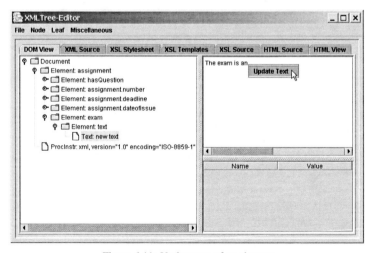

Figure 6.11: Update text of an element

Attributes can be added or removed by right-clicking in the *Attributes* part of the *DOM View* or by using the *Leaf* menu and filling in the dialog shown in Figure 6.12. When we remove an attribute, it gets the *value* "Delete" and will be removed when we save the XML document. When we delete other nodes with *Node - Delete*, these nodes get the _status="Delete" and are also removed during the next save action. We can choose between deleting with or without successor nodes.

Figure 6.12: New attribute dialog

Next, we add a comment by right-clicking on the element **exam** and choosing *Insert as Sibling - New Comment* in the popup menu to insert the comment before the exam (not shown). We write the comment into the dialog (see Figure 6.13) and press the OK button. The *XML Source* for the comment looks like shown in Figure 6.14. Analogously, we can add processing instructions.

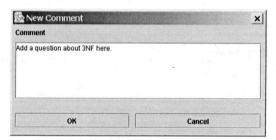

Figure 6.13: New comment dialog

We finish with saving the document (*File - Save XML to DB*), so we have the XML document shown in Figure 6.1 on page 105. When the assignment is handed out to students, it is useful to publish it in *RelAndXML* with *File - Publish Document* and then *File - Save XML to DB*. Then, the document cannot be changed any more without giving it a new version number.

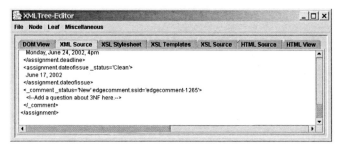

Figure 6.14: XML Source pane with comment

6.2 Working with XSLT Documents

We open and save XSL documents via the *File* menu. Figure 6.15 shows the *XSL Stylesheet* with the start tags and the end tag of a stylesheet. The *XSL Templates*, shown in Figure 6.16, lets the user flip through all the templates of the stylesheet. With the buttons at the bottom of the view, we can remove the current template from the stylesheet and add it again, we can create a new template and save or cancel changes to the template. The button *Find More Templates* lets the user search for templates in the database and add them to the current stylesheet. We can look at the source of the XSL document in the read-only *XSL Source* (see Figure 6.17).

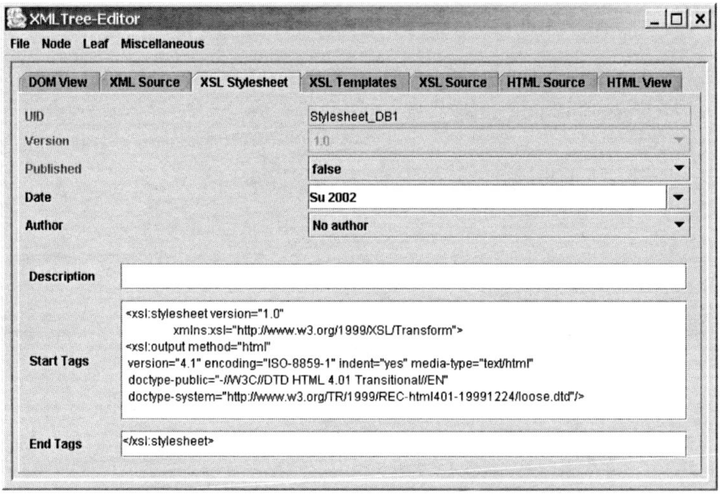

Figure 6.15: XSL Stylesheet pane

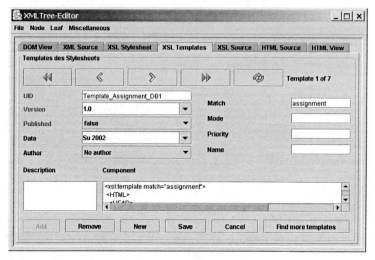

Figure 6.16: XSL Templates pane

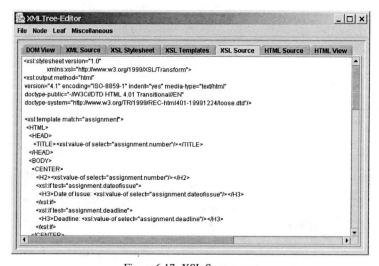

Figure 6.17: XSL Source pane

6.3   Viewing HTML Documents

When we switch to *HTML Source* (see Figure 6.18), the XSL processor takes the current XML and XSL documents as input and procudes an HTML document as output. Figure 6.19 shows the *HTML View* – the HTML output like presented in a browser. This browser view is working correctly for HTML 3.2 only, due to the limited functionality of the Java class `JEditorPane`. If the HTML view looks incorrect, we use *File - Save HTML to File* and view the document in our favorite browser. (If it still looks incorrect, we go back to our XSL document and look for errors.)

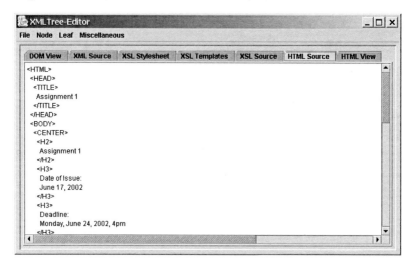

Figure 6.18: HTML Source pane

6.4   Various Features

The application has a *Protocol* window, where the SQL statements that are executed are shown. Figure 6.20 shows this window during a save action for "Assignment 1" when some elements and attributes were added.

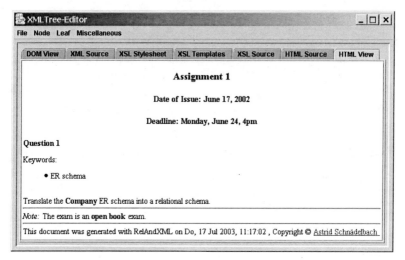

Figure 6.19: HTML View pane

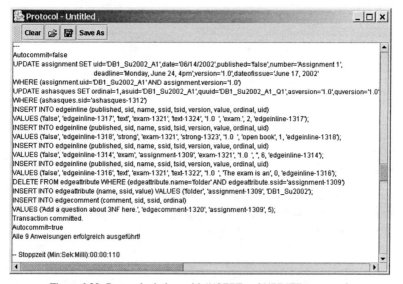

Figure 6.20: Protocol window with INSERT and UPDATE commands

The *Administration* window for the administrator contains just a few features. It is not meant to replace the tools that come with the chosen DBMS product. With the *Select* button, we can print the content of the table chosen in the combobox on the right to the *Protocol* window. With the *Run Script* button, we can run a script via JDBC. The *Generate Metadata* button is useful when the *Core* is replaced: it generates INSERT commands for some of the meta data tables. The buttons *Save Tables* and *Load Tables* are a simple possibility to backup and restore the database content from *RelAndXML*; instead of a semicolon as delimiter, we use <_raxtrenner> (it's a constant, so we can change it) such that we can use semicolons in the database content.

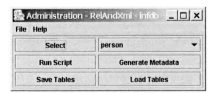

Figure 6.21: Frame for the administrator

The about box of the system is shown in Figure 6.22.

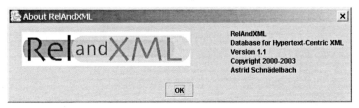

Figure 6.22: About box

6.5   Conclusion and Outlook

RelAndXML offers a user-friendly graphical user interface to work with XML, XSL, and HTML documents.

The implementation shows that the design of the database meets the requirements that we described in the Introduction.

The response time of the system is good. In our system environment with a client PC and a LAN network connection to the database server, it takes less than a second to open or save a document.

Outlook

Nevertheless, *RelAndXML* is still prototype software. In the future, one could include the following features:

- The menus in the *DOM View* should be context-sensitive. For instance, on a right-click on a text node, they should not show the *Insert as Child* menu item.

- The *Node* menu should have the items *Update Assignment*, *Update Question*, etc. that open dialogs similar to the *Open ...* and *DB ...* dialogs and offer a more convenient way to change the values of text modules.

- The search parts of the "Open from database" dialogs should be extended such that the user does not have to write SQL statements.

Chapter 7

Implementation of RelAndXML

In this chapter, we describe the implementation of *RelAndXML*. We start with a section about the system architecture. In the second section, we describe the applied technologies: Java with the DOM parser Xerces, the XSL processor Xalan, and the database access with JDBC. In the third section, we describe the implementation of the graphical user interface for the DOM documents. The fourth section explains the algorithm Rel2XML which builds an XML document from the relational data. In the fifth section, the decomposing and saving of an XML document into the relational database with the algorithm XML2Rel is explained. We conclude with an outlook to suggestions for improvement and possible extensions.

7.1 System Architecture

The Java implementation consists of the package `relandxml` having four packages `gui`, `algo`, `db`, and `utils`; see Figure 7.1.

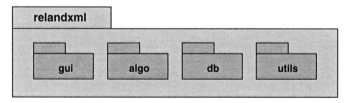

Figure 7.1: *RelAndXML* packages

Figure 7.2 gives an overview about the system with the according packages shown on the right. At the top, a schematic DOM view stands in place of the classes for the graphical user interface that we have shown in the tutorial (see Chapter 6) and that belong to the package `gui`.

In the remainder of the figure, we show classes with data structure character in square boxes with rounded corners and classes with mostly algorithmic character written along an arrow.

The package `algo` contains the main algorithms and data structures: The classes `DomToTreeModelAdapter`, `AttrToTableModelAdapter`, and `AdapterNode` are used to connect the GUI tree presentation to the underlying DOM document (see Subsection 7.2.1 and Section 7.3). The class `XMLBaum` comprises the DOM document and several objects of helper classes which are used during the assembling and decomposing of the document: `PrimaryKey` identifies the database tuple that belongs to the root element of the document. This class as well as the helper classes `ValueKnoten` and `BaumKnoten` are explained along with the algorithmic class `Rel2XML` in Section 7.4. The decomposing algorithm `XML2Rel` as well as its helper class `Datensatz` are described in Section 7.5.

The `db` package contains the classes for the database access. The class `DBAccess` has the information about the JDBC connection; it executes SQL statements and delivers the results. When the system is started, `DBAccess` fills the `MetaDatenbank` with values according to the *Metadata* tables in the database. The `MetaDatenbank` is also used by `Rel2XML` and `XML2Rel`. See also Subsection 7.2.3.

The package `util` contains a few helper classes used in the other packages.

We do not use a DOM representation of the XSL document. Instead, the *XSL Stylesheet* and the *XSL Templates* views of the *XMLTree-Editor* read and write plain strings from and to the tables in the *Presentation* schema. For the *XSL Source*, we concatenate the strings from *XSL Stylesheet* and *XSL Templates* to receive the complete stylesheet. Since this is standard programming, we do not explain it in greater detail. For the transformation to an HTML document, we use the XSL processor Xalan as explained in Subsection 7.2.2.

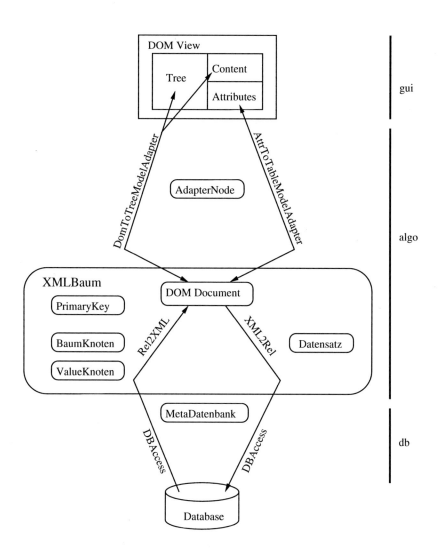

Figure 7.2: *RelAndXML* system

7.2   Applied Java Technologies

In this section, we give a brief introduction to the Java technologies applied for the implementation: the XML parser Xerces, the XSL processor Xalan, and JDBC for the database
access.

7.2.1   Handling XML Documents

For the parsing and construction of XML documents and their DOM trees, we use Xerces,
which is the XML parser of the Apache XML project. See [Xer03] for download and
installation instructions.

Parsing XML Files

The class library of Xerces includes a simple command-line program called
`sax.Counter` to check XML documents. By default, `sax.Counter` only checks for
well-formedness, the `-v` flag turns on validation. To validate the document `assign-
ment2.xml` that includes a document type declaration, we write

```
java sax.Counter -v assignment2.xml
```

In the following lines of a Java program, we check XML documents with a DOM-
Parser object from the package `org.apache.xerces.parsers`. We also import the
package `org.w3c.dom`, which includes the interfaces for the different DOM types, for
instance `Document` and `Element`[1]. We turn on the validation feature in line 6.

```
1  import org.apache.xerces.parsers.*;
2  import org.w3c.dom.*;
3  ...
4  String xmlDocument = "assignment2.xml";
5  DOMParser parser = new DOMParser();
6  parser.setFeature("http://xml.org/sax/features/validation",
7                     true);
8  parser.parse(xmlDocument);
9  Document doc = parser.getDocument();
```

If the XML document is not valid (or well-formed), Java throws a `SAXParseExcep-
tion`, which contains an error message as well as the line and column of the first error.

---

[1]The DOM types are shown in Figure 2.3 on page 22.

Creating DOM Trees

With the following lines, we explain how to create a DOM tree with Java.

```
1   import org.w3c.dom.*;
2   import org.apache.xerces.dom.*;
3   ...
4   DOMImplementation domImpl = new DOMImplementationImpl();
5   Document doc = domImpl.createDocument(namespaceURI,
6                                         rootName, docType);
7   doc.appendChild(
8     doc.createProcessingInstruction("xml",
9             "version=\"1.0\" encoding=\"ISO-8859-1\""));
10  Element root = doc.getDocumentElement();
```

The interface `DOMImplementation` is part of the package `org.w3c.dom`. We also need the Xerces-specific implementation `DOMImplementationImpl` from the package `org.apache.xerces.dom`. In line 4, we create a `DOMImplementation` object, which we use in line 5 to create a `Document` with a namespace, name of the root element and a document type declaration. The namespace and document type declaration can be `null`. In lines 7 to 9 we create the XML declaration and append it to the document. In line 10, we access the root element of the document.

The following lines show how new nodes are created. First, we create a node of type *X*, then we append it to its parent node. To an element `elt` we can also add attributes.

```
x = doc.createX(...);
elt.appendChild(x);
elt.setAttribute(name, value);
```

Among the `createX` methods, we use the following:

```
createElement(name)
createTextNode(data)
createCDATASection(data)
createComment(data)
createProcessingInstruction(target,data)
```

Traversing DOM Trees

Next, we explain how a DOM tree can be traversed with Xerces. Every node has the following (and more) methods for traversing. The methods on the left side return if there are child nodes or attributes and give access to the nodes or attributes. The methods on the right side return the DOM type of the node, its name and its value.

```
hasChildNodes()                         getNodeType()
getChildNodes()                         getNodeName()
getFirstChild()                         getNodeValue()
getNextSibling()
hasAttributes()
getAttributes()
```

The values of node name, node value, and attributes vary according to the node type as shown in Table 7.1, which is part of the Java documentation [Jav03] for `org.w3c.dom.Node`.

Interface	nodeName	nodeValue	attributes
Attr	name of attribute	value of attribute	null
CDATASection	"#cdata-section"	content of the CDATA Section	null
Comment	"#comment"	content of the comment	null
Document	"#document"	null	null
Document-Fragment	"#document-fragment"	null	null
DocumentType	document type name	null	null
Element	tag name	null	NamedNodeMap
Entity	entity name	null	null
EntityReference	name of entity referenced	null	null
Notation	notation name	null	null
Processing-Instruction	target	entire content excluding the target	null
Text	"#text"	content of the text node	null

Table 7.1: DOM node types

In the following listing, we use these methods in `decomposeNode` for decomposing a document. Starting with the document node, we decompose each node recursively and use a `switch-case` statement for the different types of nodes. The cases `Node.DOCUMENT_NODE` and `Node.ELEMENT_NODE` show how to traverse the child nodes of a node with a `for` loop (lines 8-11 and 26-32). The attributes of an element are accessed within the `Node.ELEMENT_NODE` case, also using a `for` loop (lines 17-25).

———————————————— decomposeNode ————————————————

```
 1  private static void
 2    decomposeNode(Node node, BufferedWriter writer,
 3                  String indentLevel) throws IOException {
 4    // switch on the type of the node
 5    switch (node.getNodeType()) {
 6    case Node.DOCUMENT_NODE:
 7      // recursive call for every child
 8      NodeList nodes = node.getChildNodes();
 9      for (int i = 0; i < nodes.getLength(); ++i)
10        decomposeNode(nodes.item(i), writer, "");
11      break;
12    case Node.ELEMENT_NODE:
13      String name = node.getNodeName();
14      writer.write(indentLevel + "Element: " + name);
15      writer.newLine();
16      // walk through attributes
17      NamedNodeMap attributes = node.getAttributes();
18      for (int i = 0; i < attributes.getLength(); ++i) {
19        Node current = attributes.item(i);
20        writer.write(indentLevel + "Attribute: "
21          + current.getNodeName() +
22          "=\"" + current.getNodeValue() + "\"");
23        writer.newLine();
24      }
25      // recursive call for every child
26      NodeList children = node.getChildNodes();
27      for (int i = 0; i < children.getLength(); ++i) {
28        decomposeNode(children.item(i), writer,
29                      indentLevel + INDENT);
30        writer.newLine();
31      }
32      break;
```

```
33   case Node.TEXT_NODE:
34       writer.write(indentLevel + "TextNode: "
35                       + node.getNodeValue());
36       break;
37   case Node.CDATA_SECTION_NODE:
38       writer.write(indentLevel + "CDATASection: "
39                       + node.getNodeValue());
40       break;
41   case Node.COMMENT_NODE:
42       writer.write(indentLevel + "Comment: "
43                       + node.getNodeValue());
44       break;
45   case Node.PROCESSING_INSTRUCTION_NODE:
46       writer.write(indentLevel + "Processing Instruction: "
47                       + node.getNodeName() +
48                       " " + node.getNodeValue() );
49       break;
50   default:
51     writer.write("***** Ignoring node: "
52                     + node.getClass().getName());
53   }
54 }
55 /** Indentation */
56 private static final String INDENT = "   ";
```
——————————————— decomposeNode ———————————————

Serialization

The transformation of a DOM tree to an XML document is called *serialization*. It can be done analogously to the listing above, but it is easier to use the Xerces-specific XMLSerializer from the package org.apache.xml.serialize or the implementation-independent javax.xml.transform.Transformer. In the following lines, we show how to use TransformerFactory to get a Transformer. We can set some output properties like the method ("xml", "html", "text"), the encoding (set to "ISO-8859-1" for German umlauts) and the indentation. The serialization is done in lines 9 and 10. The first parameter of the transform method is the input, the second is the output. Both can be either a DOM document (classes DOMSource and DOMResult) or a stream object (classes StreamSource and StreamResult). The exception TransformerEx-

`ception` has to be caught. The classes are in the packages `javax.xml.transform`, `javax.xml.transform.stream`, and `javax.xml.transform.dom`.

```
1   Document doc = ...;
2   TransformerFactory transFactory
3                   = TransformerFactory.newInstance();
4   Transformer transformer = transFactory.newTransformer();
5   transformer.setOutputProperty(OutputKeys.METHOD, "xml");
6   transformer.setOutputProperty(OutputKeys.ENCODING,
7                           "ISO-8859-1");
8   transformer.setOutputProperty(OutputKeys.INDENT, "yes");
9   transformer.transform(new DOMSource(doc),
10                  new StreamResult(outputFilename));
```

7.2.2 Handling XSL Documents

For the processing of XSL documents, we use Xalan which is the XSLT processor of the Apache XML project [Xal03]. To use Xalan as a command line processor, pass the input file, stylesheet file, and output file as shown here:

```
java org.apache.xalan.xslt.Process -in <input.xml>
-xsl <transform.xsl> -out <output.html>
```

Xalan can be used within Java with a `Transformer` object similar to the one for Xerces. The difference is the constructor of the `Transformer`: it gets the XSL stylesheet as parameter.

```
1   Document doc = ...;
2   String xslFile = ...;
3   String htmlFile = ...;
4   TransformerFactory tFactory
5                   = TransformerFactory.newInstance();
6   Transformer transformer = tFactory.newTransformer(
7                       new StreamSource(
8                           new FileReader(xslFile)));
9   transformer.transform(new DOMSource(doc),
10                  new StreamResult(htmlFile);
```

7.2.3   Database Access with JDBC and the Metadata

JDBC provides database access from Java programs that is independent from a specific object-relational database product. This works with JDBC drivers which are available for almost all database products. After establishing a connection to a (possibly remote) database server, JDBC passes SQL statements to it and returns result messages (e.g. for INSERT and UPDATE commands) or result sets (for SELECT commands). The result sets have methods to walk through the rows and to access the values of each row.

Since JDBC is widely in use, we refrain from explaining code examples here. For further information, see [HC02, JDB03].

In *RelAndXML*, the class `DBAccess` is concerned with the JDBC access and it also manages the `MetaDatenbank` that contains the information from the *Metadata* tables in the database. When *RelAndXML* is started, `DBAccess` reads the URL of the database and the location of the JDBC driver from a properties file and fills the `MetaDatenbank` with information. In this way, *RelAndXML* does not have to access the database every-time, some metadata information is needed (and this information is needed constantly). Figure 7.3 shows the structure of the `MetaDatenbank`. It contains a hash map (a subclass of `java.util.HashMap`) with one `MetaTabelle` object for each table in the *Core*, *Extension*, and *Presentation* part of the database.

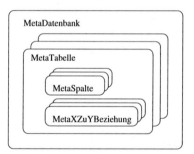

Figure 7.3: Class `MetaDatenbank`

Each `MetaTabelle` object has the information from the table RaxMetaTable and also contains some hash maps: one for the `MetaSpalte` objects and several for the relationship objects. There is a `MetaSpalte` object for each column of the table. It contains the information from the metadata table RaxMetaColumn. Then there are `HashMaps` for 1:1, 1:N, and M:N relationships with the information from the tables RaxMeta1ToOne, RaxMetaOneToN, and RaxMetaMToN respectively.   The structure of these metadata objects is analogous to the ER schema shown in Subsection 5.4.1 on page 99. For instance, each column object is associated to its table object, and each relationship object has access to the involved column or table objects.

7.3   A Graphical User Interface for a DOM Tree

As we have seen in the tutorial in Chapter 6, *RelAndXML* has a GUI with a tree representation that provides methods to update the tree by adding, changing or deleting parts of it. In this subsection, we explain how the underlying DOM tree and the GUI are connected.

Figure 7.4 shows the *DOM View* pane of the *XMLTree-Editor* window. The left side, called *Tree*, shows the DOM tree with a JTree object. The upper right side, called *Content*, displays the content or name of the selected node. Since attributes are not included as children in the DOM hierarchy, we display them in a JTable object in the lower right side called *Attributes*, if the selected node is an element.

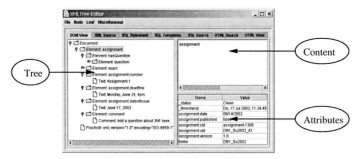

Figure 7.4: XMLTree-Editor – DOM View pane

We follow the description in [A⁺01], which allows the display of a DOM as a JTree. Then, we extend it using some information of [ASW01] such that modifications of the JTree are done in the DOM tree also. We also set a status flag which makes it possible to transfer the modifications to the database.

7.3.1   Displaying a DOM Tree

A JTree object is able to display a TreeModel. Therefore, we need an adapter class AdapterNode to wrap each DOM node and a class DomToTreeModelAdapter which implements the interface TreeModel. Both classes are part of the relandxml.algo package.

The class AdapterNode declares a variable domNode to hold the DOM Node. The methods of AdapterNode pass requests to the domNode by calling its methods (see Subsection 7.2.1). The `toString` method is used for the representation of the Tree in the DOM view and prints the node type, possibly followed by its name or value (see Table 7.1).

```
———————————————————————— AdapterNode ————————————————————————
 1  public class AdapterNode {
 2    private org.w3c.dom.Node domNode;
 3    private static final String[] typeName = {
 4      "none", "Element", "Attr", "Text", "CDATA", "EntityRef",
 5      "Entity", "ProcInstr", "Comment", "Document",
 6      "DocType", "DocFragment", "Notation"
 7    };
 8
 9    public AdapterNode(org.w3c.dom.Node node)
10                                        throws DOMException {
11      domNode = node;
12    }
13
14    public String toString() {
15      String s = typeName[domNode.getNodeType()];
16      String nodeName = domNode.getNodeName();
17      if (! nodeName.startsWith("#")) {
18        s += ": " + nodeName;
19      }
20      if (domNode.getNodeValue() != null) {
21        if (s.startsWith("ProcInstr"))
22          s += ", ";
23        else
24          s += ": ";
25        // Trim the value to get rid of NL's at the front
26        String t = domNode.getNodeValue().trim();
27        int x = t.indexOf("\n");
28        if (x >= 0)
29          t = t.substring(0, x);
30        s += t;
31      }
32      return s;
33    }
34    ...
35  }
———————————————————————— AdapterNode ————————————————————————
```

The following `content` method is used for the Content part of the DOM view and either prints the node name or its value.

─────────────────────────── Class AdapterNode ───────────────────────────

```
1   public String content() {
2       String s = "";
3       switch (domNode.getNodeType()) {
4         case Node.DOCUMENT_TYPE_NODE:
5           s += domNode.getNodeName();
6           break;
7         case Node.ELEMENT_NODE:
8           s += domNode.getNodeName();
9           break;
10        case Node.COMMENT_NODE: // fall through
11        case Node.CDATA_SECTION_NODE: // fall through
12        case Node.TEXT_NODE:
13          s += domNode.getNodeValue();
14          break;
15        case Node.ENTITY_NODE: //fall through
16        case Node.ENTITY_REFERENCE_NODE:
17          s += domNode.getNodeName();
18          break;
19      }
20      return s;
21  }
```

─────────────────────────── Class AdapterNode ───────────────────────────

We also add the following three methods, which are called by the `TreeModel` adapter. They return the index of a specified child, the child that corresponds to a given index, and the count of child nodes.

─────────────────────────── Class AdapterNode ───────────────────────────

```
1   public int index(AdapterNode child) {
2       int count = childCount();
3       for (int i=0; i<count; i++) {
4         AdapterNode n = this.child(i);
5         if (child.domNode == n.domNode) return i;
6       }
7       return -1; // Should never get here.
8   }
9
```

```
10    public AdapterNode child(int searchIndex) {
11      return new AdapterNode(
12            domNode.getChildNodes().item(searchIndex));
13    }
14    public int childCount() {
15        return domNode.getChildNodes().getLength();
16    }
```
———————————————— Class AdapterNode ————————————————

We will add more methods to AdapterNode in this section, but first, we define the
DomToTreeModelAdapter, which converts the current DOM document into a JTree
model. Since DomToTreeModelAdapter implements the interface of javax.swing.
tree.TreeModel, it has to implement the following methods:

———————————————— Interface TreeModel ————————————————
```
1  public Object   getRoot();
2  public boolean  isLeaf(Object node);
3  public int      getChildCount(Object parent);
4  public Object   getChild(Object parent, Object child);
5  public int      getIndexOfChild(Object parent,
6                                       Object child);
7  public void     valueForPathChanged(TreePath path,
8                                       Object newValue);
9  void addTreeModelListener(TreeModelListener l);
10 void removeTreeModelListener(TreeModelListener l);
```
———————————————— Interface TreeModel ————————————————

In DomToTreeModelAdapter, the getRoot method returns the root node of the
document, wrapped as an AdapterNode object. JTree uses the isLeaf method to
determine whether or not to display a clickable expand/contract icon to the left of the node,
so this method returns true only if the node has children. The methods getChildCount,
getChild, and getIndexOfChild are straightforward.

———————————————— Class DomToTreeModelAdapter ————————————————
```
1  public class DomToTreeModelAdapter
2                  implements javax.swing.tree.TreeModel {
3    private org.w3c.dom.Document document;
4
5    public DomToTreeModelAdapter(Document document) {
6      this.document = document;
7    }
```

```
8    public Object getRoot() {
9      return rootNode;
10   }
11
12   public boolean isLeaf(Object aNode) {
13     AdapterNode node = (AdapterNode) aNode;
14     if (node.childCount() > 0)
15       return false;
16     return true;
17   }
18
19   public int getChildCount(Object parent) {
20     AdapterNode node = (AdapterNode) parent;
21     return node.childCount();
22   }
23
24   public Object getChild(Object parent, int index) {
25     AdapterNode node = (AdapterNode) parent;
26     return node.child(index);
27   }
28
29   public int getIndexOfChild(Object parent, Object child) {
30     AdapterNode node = (AdapterNode) parent;
31     return node.index((AdapterNode) child);
32   }
33 }
```

———————————— Class DomToTreeModelAdapter ——————————

Now, we add the code to construct an adapter and deliver it to the JTree as the TreeModel:

```
JTree tree = new JTree(new DomToTreeModelAdapter());
```

7.3.2 Adding or Updating Nodes

Listeners and Events

The following methods are needed to change the document. After any change to the underlying model, we need to inform all the listeners that a change had occurred. To inform listeners, we need the ability to register them.

─────────────── Class DomToTreeModelAdapter ───────────────

```
1  private LinkedList listenerList = new LinkedList();
2  public void addTreeModelListener(TreeModelListener listener) {
3    if (listener!=null && !listenerList.contains(listener)) {
4      listenerList.add( listener );
5    }
6  }
7  public void removeTreeModelListener(
8                            TreeModelListener listener) {
9    if (listener!=null) {
10     listenerList.remove ( listener );
11   }
12 }
```

─────────────── Class DomToTreeModelAdapter ───────────────

When the `JTree` component is created, it registers itself with the model as a `TreeModelListener`. Therefore, the `TreeModel` is expected to perform the following notifications, which are defined in `swing.event.TreeModelListener`.

─────────────── Interface TreeModelListener ───────────────

```
1  void treeNodesChanged (TreeModelEvent e);
2  void treeNodesInserted (TreeModelEvent e);
3  void treeNodesRemoved (TreeModelEvent e);
4  void treeStructureChanged (TreeModelEvent e);
```

─────────────── Interface TreeModelListener ───────────────

A `TreeModelEvent` encapsulates information describing the changes to the tree model. Depending on the type of notification, we use one of the following constructors of `TreeModelEvent`:

─────────────── Class TreeModelEvent ───────────────

```
1  public TreeModelEvent(Object source, TreePath path) {...};
2  public TreeModelEvent(Object source, TreePath path,
3                    int[] childIndices,
4                    Object[] children) {...};
```

─────────────── Class TreeModelEvent ───────────────

In our case, the `source` argument is the `DomToTreeModelAdapter` object. The path argument points to the *parent* of the changes. For instance, if nodes were inserted, the path points to the parent node under which the inserts took place. (A `TreePath` represents a path to a node with an array containing all the nodes from the root to that node.)

The first constructor does not specify children and is used when making a structure-changed notification. We use this constructor in the method `valueForPathChanged` on page 138. When making a nodes-changed, nodes-inserted, or nodes-removed notification, the second constructor is used. Children are specified as indexes under a single parent. Changes to multiple nodes require multiple notifications. We usually only have a single child, whose index and node we have to convert to an array, see the methods `insert-NodeInto` and `insertNodeBefore` starting on page 139.

The methods of `TreeModelListener` are called from the following methods in `DomToTreeModelAdapter`, which are invoked whenever we need to notify `JTree` listeners of a change.

```
———————————— Class DomToTreeModelAdapter ————————————
1   public void fireTreeNodesChanged( TreeModelEvent e ) {
2       Iterator listeners = listenerList.iterator();
3       while ( listeners.hasNext() ) {
4         TreeModelListener listener
5            = (TreeModelListener) listeners.next();
6         listener.treeNodesChanged( e );
7       }
8   }
9
10  public void fireTreeNodesInserted( TreeModelEvent e ) {
11      Iterator listeners = listenerList.iterator();
12      while ( listeners.hasNext() ) {
13        TreeModelListener listener
14           = (TreeModelListener) listeners.next();
15        listener.treeNodesInserted( e );
16      }
17  }
18
19  public void fireTreeNodesRemoved( TreeModelEvent e ) {
20      Iterator listeners = listenerList.iterator();
21      while ( listeners.hasNext() ) {
22        TreeModelListener listener
```

```
23          = (TreeModelListener) listeners.next();
24       listener.treeNodesRemoved( e );
25     }
26   }
27
28   public void fireTreeStructureChanged( TreeModelEvent e ) {
29     Iterator listeners = listenerList.iterator();
30     while ( listeners.hasNext() ) {
31       TreeModelListener listener
32          = (TreeModelListener) listeners.next();
33       listener.treeStructureChanged( e );
34     }
35   }
```
———————————— Class DomToTreeModelAdapter ————————————

Status of Nodes

As mentioned in the tutorial, we use an attribute _status when making changes in the tree. This status is set via the class AdapterNode. The status of each node decides in XML2Rel, whether an INSERT, UPDATE, or DELETE command is generated.

———————————— Class AdapterNode ————————————
```
1  public static final String RAX_STATUS   = "_status";
2  public static final String RAX_CLEAN    = "Clean";
3  public static final String RAX_READONLY = "ReadOnly";
4  public static final String RAX_NEW      = "New";
5  public static final String RAX_MODIFIED = "Modified";
6  public static final String RAX_DELETE   = "Delete";
7
8  public String getStatus() { ... };
9  protected void setStatus (String newStatus) { ... };
```
———————————— Class AdapterNode ————————————

When a document is loaded from the database, its modifiable nodes get the status "Clean" and the not changeable elements the status "ReadOnly". Elements that are inserted via the GUI are "New". When a child node or attribute of a node is added, modified or removed, the setStatus method in AdapterNode is called with the claimed status "Modified". It sets the status as shown in the following table.

Current Status	+	Claimed Status	=	New Status
"New"		"Modified"		"New"
"Clean"		"Modified"		"Modified"
"ReadOnly"		"Modified"		throws Exception
"Delete"		"Modified"		"Delete"

When the status is "ReadOnly", the user is not allowed to make changes to that node. When the user wants to delete nodes, only new nodes are deleted immediately. Other nodes are marked with the status "Delete" and removed after the next save action.

Current Status	+	Claimed Status	=	New Status
"New"		"Delete"		remove from tree
"Clean"		"Delete"		"Delete"
"ReadOnly"		"Delete"		"ReadOnly"
"Modified"		"Delete"		"Delete"

Next, we extend AdapterNode with an update and a replaceChild method which are used to change the value of a node. They change the status to "Modified" with the method setStatus.

——————————————— Class AdapterNode ———————————————

```
1  public void update(Object newVal, AdapterNode parent) {
2      String newValue = newVal.toString();
3      int type = domNode.getNodeType();
4      if (type == Node.TEXT_NODE || type == Node.COMMENT_NODE
5          || type == Node.CDATA_SECTION_NODE) {
6        if (domNode.getNodeValue().equals(newValue))
7          return;
8        domNode.setNodeValue(newValue);
9        parent.setStatus(RAX_MODIFIED);
10      }
11      if (type == Node.ELEMENT_NODE) {
12        if (childCount() == 0) {
13          AdapterNode newNode = new AdapterNode(document,
14                                                newValue);
15          parent.replaceChild(newNode, this);
16          domNode = newNode.domNode;
17          setStatus(RAX_MODIFIED);
18        }
19        else {
```

```
20          String message = "You can only rename elements that
21                          do not have any child nodes.";
22          throw new RelAndXMLException(message);
23      }
24    }
25  }
26
27  public void replaceChild (AdapterNode newChild,
28                            AdapterNode oldChild) {
29    domNode.replaceChild(newChild.domNode, oldChild.domNode);
30    setStatus(RAX_MODIFIED);
31  }
```
———————————————— Class AdapterNode ————————————————

The update method of AdapterNode is used in DomToTreeModelAdapter in the
method valueForPathChanged which is shown below. It notifies its listeners (the
JTree) of the change by calling fireTreeNodesChanged. Now we have completed
the implementation of the interface TreeModel.

———————————————— Class DomToTreeModelAdapter ————————————————
```
1  public void valueForPathChanged(TreePath path,
2                                  Object newValue) {
3    AdapterNode node
4      = (AdapterNode)path.getLastPathComponent();
5    TreePath parentPath = path.getParentPath();
6    AdapterNode parent
7      = (AdapterNode)parentPath.getLastPathComponent();
8    node.update(newValue, parent);
9    fireTreeNodesChanged(
10     new TreeModelEvent(this, parentPath));
11 }
```
———————————————— Class DomToTreeModelAdapter ————————————————

The following methods for AdapterNode are used for the insertion of nodes.

———————————————— Class AdapterNode ————————————————
```
1  public void appendChildNode (AdapterNode node) {
2    domNode.appendChild(node.domNode);
3    setStatus(RAX_MODIFIED);
4  }
```

```
5   public void insertBefore (AdapterNode newNode,
6                             AdapterNode oldNode) {
7     domNode.insertBefore(newNode.domNode, oldNode.domNode);
8     setStatus(RAX_MODIFIED);
9   }
```
——————————————— Class AdapterNode ———————————————

In DomToTreeModelAdapter, the method insertNodeInto inserts a new child node into the node. The method insertBeforeNode inserts a new sibling node before the node. At the end of the methods, we fire fireTreeNodesInserted(evt) to notify the underlying tree.

——————————————— Class DomToTreeModelAdapter ———————————————
```
1   public TreePath insertNodeInto (int type,AdapterNode node,
2                                   TreePath path)
3                                       throws DOMException{
4     if (RAX_READONLY.equals(node.getStatus())) {
5       throw new RelAndXMLException(readOnlyMsg);
6     }
7     switch (node.getW3CNodeType()) {
8     case Node.DOCUMENT_NODE: //fall through
9     case Node.ELEMENT_NODE:
10      AdapterNode child = new AdapterNode(document, type);
11      node.appendChildNode(child);
12      int[] index = {node.childCount()};
13      Object[] children = {child};
14      TreeModelEvent evt
15        = new TreeModelEvent(this, path, index, children);
16      fireTreeNodesInserted(evt);
17      return path.pathByAddingChild(child);
18    default:
19      throw new RelAndXMLException(noChildrenMsg);
20    }
21  }
22
23  public TreePath insertNodeBefore (int type, AdapterNode
24                                    oldNode, TreePath path) {
25    AdapterNode parentNode
26      = (AdapterNode)path.getLastPathComponent();
27    String nodeStatus = parentNode.getStatus();
```

```
28    if (RAX_READONLY.equals(nodeStatus)) {
29      throw new RelAndXMLException(readOnlyParentMsg);
30    }
31    switch (parentNode.getW3CNodeType()) {
32      case Node.DOCUMENT_NODE: // fall through
33      case Node.ELEMENT_NODE:
34        AdapterNode newNode
35          = new AdapterNode(document, type);
36        parentNode.insertBefore(newNode, oldNode);
37        int index[] = {parentNode.index(oldNode)};
38        Object[] children = {newNode};
39        TreeModelEvent evt
40          = new TreeModelEvent(this, path, index, children);
41        fireTreeNodesInserted(evt);
42        return path.pathByAddingChild(newNode);
43      default:
44        throw new RelAndXMLException(noChildrenMsg);
45    }
46  }
```
———————————— Class DomToTreeModelAdapter ————————————

7.3.3 Deleting Nodes

For the deletion of nodes, we add a method `removeChild` to `AdapterNode` that removes
the child and then sets the status of the node.

———————————— Class AdapterNode ————————————
```
1  public void removeChild (AdapterNode node) {
2      if (RAX_READONLY.equals(getStatus()))
3        return;
4      domNode.removeChild(node.domNode);
5      if (domNode.getNodeType() == Node.ELEMENT_NODE) {
6        setStatus(RAX_MODIFIED);
7      }
8  }
```
———————————— Class AdapterNode ————————————

Changes of the DOM tree are only transferred to the database when a save action is
performed. Therefore, we cannot actually delete nodes immediately, since they would not
be deleted in the database later. The `deleteNode` method in `DomToTreeModelAdapter`
sets the status of nodes that are to be deleted to `"Delete"` and leaves them in the tree.

The parameter deep decides whether all successive nodes are deleted also. An exception are nodes with the status "New": they have not been inserted into the database, so they can be deleted immediately.

```
───────────────── Class DomToTreeModelAdapter ─────────────────
 1  public boolean deleteNode (AdapterNode deleteNode,
 2                              TreePath path, boolean deep) {
 3     AdapterNode parent = deleteNode.getParentNode();
 4     String delStatus = deleteNode.getStatus();
 5     int[] index = {getIndexOfChild(parent, deleteNode)};
 6     Object[] children = {deleteNode};
 7     if (AdapterNode.RAX_CLEAN.equals(delStatus)
 8        ||AdapterNode.RAX_MODIFIED.equals(delStatus)) {
 9        deleteNode.setStatus(AdapterNode.RAX_DELETE, deep);
10        deleteNode.getParentNode().setStatus(
11                              AdapterNode.RAX_MODIFIED);
12        TreeModelEvent evt
13          = new TreeModelEvent(this, path, index, children);
14        fireTreeNodesChanged(evt);
15        return false;
16     }
17     else if (AdapterNode.RAX_NEW.equals(delStatus)) {
18        parent.removeChild(deleteNode);
19        TreeModelEvent evt
20          = new TreeModelEvent(this, path, index, children);
21        fireTreeNodesRemoved(evt);
22        return true;
23     }
24     else
25        throw new RelAndXMLException("Cannot delete node "
26                              + deleteNode);
27  }
───────────────── Class DomToTreeModelAdapter ─────────────────
```

7.3.4 Displaying and Changing Attributes

To display and change the attributes of element nodes, we use a JTable with two columns: the first for the attributes names, the second for the attribute values. The class Attr-ToTableModelAdapter, which implements javax.swing.table.TableModel, is the equivalent to `DomToTreeModelAdapter`. The interface `TableModel` has the following methods.

```
———————————————— Interface TableModel ————————————
1  public int getColumnCount();
2  public int getRowCount();
3  public Object getValueAt(int row, int column);
4  public void setValueAt(Object newValue, int row,
5                         int column);
6  public boolean isCellEditable(int row, int column);
7  public String getColumnName(int column);
8  public Class getColumnClass(int column);
9  public void addTableModelListener(
10                 TableModelListener listener);
11 public void removeTableModelListener(
12                 TableModelListener listener);
13 public void fireTableDataChanged();
——————————————— Interface TableModel ————————————
```

For space reasons, we do not show the implementation of these methods in `Attr-ToTableModelAdapter`, but they are straightforward and make use of some additional methods in `AdapterNode` that we show next.

```
———————————————— Class AdapterNode ————————————
1  public int attributeCount() {
2    if (domNode.getNodeType()==Node.ELEMENT_NODE)
3      return domNode.getAttributes().getLength();
4    else
5      return 0;
6  }
7
8  public String getAttributeName(int i) {
9    String s = "";
10   if (domNode.getNodeType()==Node.ELEMENT_NODE) {
11     NamedNodeMap attrs = domNode.getAttributes();
12     if (i>=0 || i < attrs.getLength())
13       s = attrs.item(i).getNodeName();
14   }
15   return s;
16 }
17
```

```
18   public String getAttributeValue(int i) {
19     String s = "";
20     if (domNode.getNodeType()==Node.ELEMENT_NODE) {
21       NamedNodeMap attrs = domNode.getAttributes();
22       if (i>= 0 || i < attrs.getLength())
23         s = attrs.item(i).getNodeValue();
24     }
25     return s;
26   }
27
28   public void setAttribute(String name, String newValue) {
29     if (domNode.getNodeType()!=Node.ELEMENT_NODE)
30       return;
31     Element elt = (Element)domNode;
32     String value = elt.getAttribute(name);
33     if (value.equals("")) {
34       elt.setAttribute(name, newValue);
35       setStatus(RAX_MODIFIED);
36     }
37     else if (!newValue.equals(value)) {
38       elt.setAttribute(name, newValue);
39       setStatus(RAX_MODIFIED);
40     }
41   }
42
43   public void removeAttribute(String name) {
44     if (domNode.getNodeType()!=Node.ELEMENT_NODE)
45       return;
46     Element elt = (Element)domNode;
47     elt.setAttribute(name, RAX_DELETE);
48   }
```
———————————————— Class AdapterNode ————————————————

To remove an attribute, its value is set to `"Delete"` such that it can be deleted during the next save action.

7.4   Rel2XML – Composing XML Documents

The algorithmic class `Rel2XML` contains methods for the assembling of the *Core* and the *Extension*. It gets as input a `PrimaryKey` object which identifies a unique database tuple and assembles a DOM document from this starting point by checking all the *Core* and *Extension* tables for related tuples and following the principle of breadth search. Dynamic data structures like hash maps and dynamic arrays are used in the classes `BaumKnoten` and `ValueKnoten` in order to minimize the number of database accesses.

The algorithm is explained with the running example "Assignment 1", whose XML source is shown in Listing 2.6 on page 20. The database tuples for this assignment are shown in the Tables 5.1 on page 90 and 5.2 on page 94. The algorithm gets as input a `PrimaryKey` object with the table name and the primary key. In our example, we have a `PrimaryKey` object with the attributes

```
──────────── PrimaryKey for "Assignment 1" ────────────
tabName = "assignment"
systemId = "assignment-1"
attributes = {uid="DB1_Su2002_A1", version="1.0"}
──────────────────────────────────────────────────────
```

Our aim is to get a DOM tree of the document which we represent as shown in Figure 7.5. For a shorter notation, we omit attribute nodes, text nodes and child *Core* nodes. Ordinal attributes are shown in squared boxes.

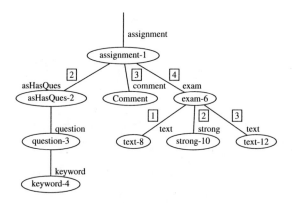

Figure 7.5: XML tree for "Assignment 1"

There are three main steps in the algorithm:

1. Assemble the *Core* nodes using their identifiers only.

2. Assemble the *Extension* nodes, using identifiers only for extension table nodes.

3. Fill the *Core* and *Extension* nodes with data.

The table name will be the XML root element. Note that any table name from the *Core* schema can serve as root element. From there the algorithm builds SELECT statements dynamically according to the metadata in `MetaDatenbank`.

The class `BaumKnoten` is a subclass of `HashMap`. The keys are the `PrimaryKey` objects for the nodes, and the values have type `ArrayList`. We use two objects `erwKnoten` and `neuKnoten` of this class to save nodes that will be considered again during the algorithm.

The class `ValueKnoten` is a subclass of `HashMap` as well. There, the keys are table names and the values are of type `BaumKnoten`. An object `kernKnoten` of this class is used while assembling the *Core*. An instance `valueKnoten` of this class is used to save nodes, whose data has to be loaded from a node table. This way, each node table is accessed at most once.

7.4.1 Assembling the Core

At the start, the `kernKnoten` object contains a `BaumKnoten` object for the table **Assignment** and the node with the sid `"assignment-1"`. We represent the `PrimaryKey` object by its `systemId` and the node by drawing an oval around it.

```
kernKnoten=ValueKnoten[
    "assignment"=BaumKnoten{"assignment-1" →( assignment-1 )}
                    ]
```

For each entry in `kernKnoten`, `Rel2XML` checks the `MetaDatenbank` for relationships to the table in the key of the entry (`"assignment"` here) and dynamically builds SELECT statements to look for tuples in related tables whose foreign key columns match the values of the `PrimaryKey` objects. In our example, we get three queries since the table **Assignment** is associated with **Course**, **Person**, and **Question**. The queries look somewhat verbose and generous with parentheses, because the generating methods work for all cases, especially for reflexive relationships.

```
 1   SELECT a.sid AS asid, b.version AS bversion,b.uid AS buid, b.sid AS bsid,
 2           b.courseuid AS bcourseuid,b.courseversion AS bcourseversion
 3   FROM   assignment AS b, course AS a
 4   WHERE ((b.version='1.0' AND b.uid='DB1_Su2002_A1'))
 5           AND (a.uid=b.courseuid AND a.version=b.courseversion)
 6
 7   SELECT a.sid AS asid, b.version AS bversion,b.uid AS buid, b.sid AS  bsid,
 8           b.authoruid AS bauthoruid,b.authorversion AS bauthorversion
 9   FROM assignment AS b, person AS a
10   WHERE ((b.version='1.0' AND b.uid='DB1_Su2002_A1'))
11           AND (a.uid=b.authoruid AND a.version=b.authorversion)
12
13   SELECT ashasques.quuid,ashasques.sid,ashasques.asversion,
14           ashasques.asuid,ashasques.quversion,ashasques.ordinal,
15           ashasques.sid AS ashasquessid, question.sid AS questionsid
16   FROM ashasques, question
17   WHERE ((ashasques.asuid='DB1_Su2002_A1'
18           AND ashasques.asversion='1.0'))
19           AND (question.uid=ashasques.quuid
20           AND question.version=ashasques.quversion)
21   ORDER BY ordinal
```

Only the last of these SQL statements gives a result containing a single question. XML elements and attributes are created in the DOM tree for this tuple (see Figure 7.6). For the usual case with several questions, we order them with an ORDER BY clause. We might as well order them with an XSL stylesheet, but that has the disadvantage that only the *HTML View* pane shows the correct order but not the *DOM View* pane.

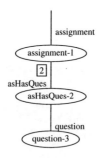

Figure 7.6: XML tree for "Assignment 1" – *Core* completed

The `PrimaryKey` for `"question-3"` is saved in `kernKnoten` for the next step within the *Core*.

```
kernKnoten=ValueKnoten[
    "question"=BaumKnoten{"question-3"→( question-3 )}
                ]
```

Furthermore, the `PrimaryKey` objects for `"assignment-1"` and `"question-3"` are saved in the `BaumKnoten` object `erwKnoten`, which will be used when assembling the *Extension*.

```
erwKnoten = BaumKnoten  {"assignment-1"→( assignment-1 ),
                        "question-3"→( question-3 )}
```

Next, we search for nodes associated to the ones in `kernKnoten`, but there are no results, such that the recursion for the assembling of the *Core* comes to an end. The cycle free insertion graph for the *Metadata* (see Figure 5.9 on page 101) is very important here. It guarantees that the recursion stops.

Due to the hypertext-centric design, we can assemble not only assignments, but other documents as well. If we open a course, for example, we get a document with the course information, information about the lecturer, and the user identifiers and versions of all the assignments and examinations. This is a distinctive feature of *RelAndXML*.

The number of SELECT statements needed to assemble the *Core* is mostly dependent on the number of tables and foreign key relationships, and not on the depth of the tree (except for reflexive relationships). This means that a large collection of questions does not need more SELECT statements than an assignment with a single question.

7.4.2 Assembling the Extension

For assembling the *Extension*, we look recursively for tuples in the tables Edge and Edgelnline that are related to the nodes in `neuKnoten` which is a copy of `erwKnoten` at the start of the recursion.

```
neuKnoten = BaumKnoten  {"assignment-1"→( assignment-1 ),
                        "question-3"→( question-3 )}
```

```
1    SELECT * FROM Edge
2    WHERE ssid IN ('assignment-1','question-3')
3    ORDER BY ssid, ordinal;
4
5    SELECT * FROM EdgeInline
6    WHERE ssid IN ('assignment-1','question-3')
7    ORDER BY ssid, ordinal;
```

As during the assembling of the *Core* we use an ORDER BY clause, such that the elements in the *DOM View* are ordered as much as possible.

The result contains the identifiers `"keyword-4"` from the Edge table and `"exam-6"` from the EdgeInline table. They are added to `erwKnoten` and the object `neuKnoten` is changed to the nodes `"keyword-4"` and `"exam-6"`.

This step has to be repeated recursively until the result set is empty. The number of SELECT statements is $2 * (L + 1)$ where L is the longest path of a *Core* node to a leaf of the tree. Figure 7.7 shows the tree after the completion of step 2.

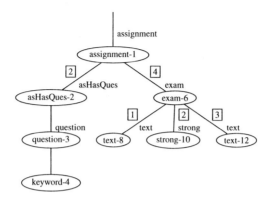

Figure 7.7: XML tree after Step 2

If the DBMS supports recursive SQL (see Subsection 3.3.3 on page 48), we can re-place these $2 * (L + 1)$ statements by the single statement shown in Listing 7.1.

The initial query (lines 4 to 14) has two subqueries connected by UNION ALL. It delivers those child nodes of the *Core* nodes that are saved in Edge or in EdgeInline. The child nodes are marked with level 1. The recursive query (lines 16 to 26) is also built by two subqueries and a UNION ALL. It delivers child nodes of those nodes found in the last step. The level is increased by 1 for every recursive call.[2] The finiteness of the recursive query is assured by restricting the level by 10000 (or any constant that is surely greater than any forthcoming depth). The actual query in line 28 orders and lists all the tuples. The result of this query is shown in Table 7.2. The DOM tree is built successively from this data.

The integration of searching in Edge and EdgeInline in one query assures that children of Edge-nodes contained in EdgeInline (and vice versa) are also found.

Assuming all XML fragments were saved in the EdgeInline table, this query shows a way of constructing a document from this table with a single SQL statement. This is not included in [FK99a, FK99b] and to our best knowledge has not been described elsewhere.

---

[2]Note that the level is not the depth in the tree, since the recursion is started with nodes of different depth.

Listing 7.1 Recursive query for Edge and EdgeInline

```
1   WITH RECURSIVE Treedata(level, sid, ssid, tsid, uid, version, published,
2                                        ordinal, name, value, tabname) AS
3   (
4       (   SELECT 1, sid, ssid, tsid, " as uid, " as version, " as published,
5                    ordinal, name, " as value, 'edge' as tabname
6           FROM Edge
7           WHERE ssid IN ('assignment-1', 'question-3')
8       UNION ALL
9           SELECT 1, sid, ssid, tsid, uid, version, published,
10                    ordinal, name, value, 'edgeinline' as tabname
11          FROM EdgeInline
12          WHERE ssid IN ('assignment-1', 'question-3')
13      )
14  UNION ALL
15      (   SELECT In.level+1, Out.sid, In.tsid, Out.tsid, ", ",
16                    ", Out.ordinal, Out.name, ", 'edge'
17          FROM Treedata In, Edge Out
18          WHERE In.tsid = Out.ssid
19      UNION ALL
20          SELECT In.level+1, Out.sid, In.tsid, Out.tsid, Out.uid, Out.version,
21                    Out.published, Out.ordinal, Out.name, Out.value, 'edgeinline'
22          FROM Treedata In, EdgeInline Out
23          WHERE In.tsid = Out.ssid AND In.level < 10000
24      )
25  )
26  SELECT * FROM Treedata ORDER BY level, ssid, ordinal;
```

Treedata					
level	**sid**	**ssid**	**tid**	**ordinal**	**name**
1	edgeinline-7	assignment-1	exam-6	4	exam
1	edge-5	question-3	keyword-4	1	keyword
2	edgeinline-9	exam-6	text-8	1	text
2	edgeinline-11	exam-6	strong-10	2	strong
2	edgeinline-13	exam-6	text-12	3	text

value	**tabname**	**uid**	**version**	**published**
	edgeinline	DB1_Su2002_Exam	1.0	false
	edge			
The exam is an	edgeinline	text-8	1.0	false
open book	edgeinline	strong-10	1.0	false
exam.	edgeinline	text-12	1.0	false

Table 7.2: Result set Treedata of the recursive query

7.4.3 Adding Data, Attributes, Comments, and Processing Instructions

The last step is to get additional tuples from the EdgeAttribute, EdgeComment, and Edge-ProcInstr tables as well as from the *ExtensionNode* tables. We also get the data for all the PrimaryKey objects in erwKnoten. In this way, there is at most one SELECT for each of these tables.

```
 1   SELECT * FROM EdgeAttribute
 2   WHERE ssid IN ('assignment-1','question-3','keyword-4',
 3                       'exam-6','text-8', 'strong-10', 'text-12');
 4   SELECT * FROM EdgeComment
 5   WHERE ssid IN ('assignment-1','question-3','keyword-4',
 6                       'exam-6','text-8', 'strong-10', 'text-12');
 7   SELECT * FROM EdgeProcInstr
 8   WHERE ssid IN ('assignment-1','question-3','keyword-4',
 9                       'exam-6','text-8', 'strong-10', 'text-12');
10   SELECT * FROM Assignment WHERE sid IN ('assignment-1');
11   SELECT * FROM Question WHERE sid IN ('question-3');
12   SELECT * FROM Keyword WHERE sid IN ('keyword-4');
```

Now, we have a complete DOM document as the one shown in Figure 7.5 on page 144.

The document is partially ordered by this time. Any additional ordering is done by an XSL processor using an XSL stylesheet.

7.5   XML2Rel – Decomposing XML Documents

The algorithm XML2Rel traverses the DOM representation of the XML document to fragment it into pieces suitable for the relational database. The fragmented data is saved in a hash map Datensatz; only when the traversing is completed, SQL statements are generated according to the content of the hash maps and the statements are executed as a single transaction.

The traversing is done like explained in Subsection 7.2.1 plus it uses the metadata in the MetaDatenbank object about the *Core* and *Extension* schemas. The root node has to be a *Core* table element. For every node, the algorithm is called recursively, checks the node and puts its data into a Datensatz object. If a node is a table node, the algorithm looks for children and attributes that are column nodes. It creates a Tabellensatz object, which is also a hash map, when the table occurs for the first time, and puts the Tabellensatz in the hash map Datensatz with the table name as key. Each Tabellensatz might contain several Zeilensatz hash maps, with a PrimaryKey object as the key. The PrimaryKey also contains the status of the node.   The Zeilensatz objects have column names as keys and the data values. Left over attributes are put in Datensatz for the table EdgeAttribute. The algorithm also looks for relationship nodes. By checking the metadata the allowed cardinality of the relationship is known. Errors in the structure like missing not-null attributes or wrong cardinalities are handled by exceptions. The edges to children corresponding to *ExtensionNode* tables are put in Datensatz for the Edge table. The remaining XML elements are marked for the EdgeInline table.

The following lines show the Tabellensatz for the table EdgeInline when "Assignment 1" is saved. The status of all nodes is "New".

```
1  datensatz = Datensatz{
2    edgeinline=Tabellensatz{
3      PrimaryKey[systemId=strong-10,raxStatus=New]
4      = Zeilensatz{value='open book', sid='edgeinline-11',
5                   tsid='strong-10', published='false',
6                   ssid='exam-6', uid='edgeinline-11',
7                   ordinal=2, name='strong', version='1.0'},
```

```
 8      PrimaryKey[systemId=text-8,raxStatus=New]
 9      = Zeilensatz{value='The exam is an',
10                     sid='edgeinline-9',
11                     tsid='text-8', published='false',
12                     ssid='exam-6', uid='edgeinline-9',
13                     ordinal=1, name='text', version='1.0'},
14      PrimaryKey[systemId=text-12,raxStatus=New]
15      = Zeilensatz{value='exam.', sid='edgeinline-13',
16                     tsid='text-12', published='false',
17                     ssid='exam-6', uid='edgeinline-13',
18                     ordinal=3, name='text', version='1.0'},
19
20      PrimaryKey[systemId=exam-6,raxStatus=New]
21      = Zeilensatz{value='', sid='edgeinline-7',
22                     tsid='exam-6', published='false',
23                     ssid='assignment-1', uid='edgeinline-7',
24                     ordinal=4, name='exam', version='1.0'}}
25    }
26    ...
27  }
```

In a second step the appropriate SQL statements are generated and executed as a single transaction. To be able to update text modules, the system must be able to generate INSERT-, UPDATE- and DELETE- statements. We found a good solution to this problem by using the internal XML attribute _status, which we explained in Section 7.3. If the _status equals "New", an INSERT statement is generated. There is an UPDATE statement for _status equals "Modified" and a DELETE statement for _status equals "Delete". If the _status equals "Clean" or "ReadOnly", no SQL statement is created. The SQL commands that are generated from the Tabellensatz above are shown in Figure 6.20 on page 116. After a successful save action all _status attributes are changed to "Clean".

7.6 Conclusion and Outlook

RelAndXML is a graphical XML editor with a tree representation on the left side and a right side divided to edit text nodes on the top and attributes on the bottom half. It is directly connected to an object-relational database system.

The entire source code was written by the author of this thesis except for two helper classes[3] and parts of the classes `DomToTreeModelAdapter` and `AdapterNode` which were taken from the technical manual [A+01]. There are approximately 25.000 lines of code in about 120 classes.

The system works well with an average response time for save and load actions of less than a second. The saving is faster, since it first disassembles the complete document and then executes the SQL statements in a single transaction. For instance, saving a new assignment with 3 questions, two parts and one additional paragraph with 12 INSERT statements takes about 220 milliseconds. For loading, SELECT statements and assembling methods are executed alternately. Loading an average assignment takes 300 to 500 milliseconds and about 30 SELECT statements. The highest loading time of the real-world documents in *InfDB* has an assignment with the questions of a complete semester – it needs about 1900 milliseconds for 36 SELECT statements.

The assembling with a recursive query is indeed faster than the non-recursive alternative. We inserted a synthetic assignment with two questions and with 100 EdgeInline elements to the database, such that each EdgeInline element is the parent of the next element. With DB2, *RelAndXML* needs 228 SELECT statements and 2.14 seconds to assemble the assignment. The recursive alternative only needs 27 SELECT statements and 1.1 seconds.

In order to make the system an even more user-friendly tool, we propose to implement the improvements suggested in the conclusion of Chapter 6.

The successful implementation proves the quality of our concept for the management and storage of hypertext-centric XML. A distinctive feature is that we can store the text modules of a document, and then assemble several documents from this data. For instance, we save the assignments of a course, and then get documents about the course and the lecturer in addition to the assignments.

---

[3]The class `ObjectAnalyzer` of the package `util` prints the values of an object and is taken from [HC03]. The class `gui.XMLDocumentWriter` which we adopted from [Fla00] is an XML serializer that indents more accurately than the one provided by Xerces.

Chapter 8

Conclusion

RelAndXML is a system that was especially designed to store and manage hypertext-centric XML documents and the according XSL stylesheets. Aspects of data-centric as well as document-centric storage approaches are combined for our hypertext-centric storage approach.

We implemented a graphical XML editor as well as the connection to an object-relational database system with Java. There are numerous XML editors (see [XEd03]) and various XML databases (see Chapter 3), but *RelAndXML* is an XML editor with a direct connection to an XML database. The requirements from Chapter 1 are fulfilled: *RelAndXML* saves XML text modules, additional XML document parts, and XSL stylesheets. It preserves document order, provides versioning and publishing of documents, and produces HTML or XHTML as output. Standard queries, especially for the search of text modules, are answered by the system.

We inserted some assignments from several courses at our institute (see Appendix B). To earn the benefits of the system, we would have to insert the complete assignments for all the courses from the previous semesters. The best thing would be to have a translator from LaTeX to XML. One thing to start with could be a tool that *assists* the user by translating a given LaTeX document into an XML document that, afterwards, could be adjusted by a human user. Such a tool would be a nice extension to *RelAndXML*.

Appendix A

Create Commands for InfDB

In this appendix, we show the CREATE commands for the *InfDB* database as we ran them on the PostgreSQL DBMS. The only expected difference when switching to another DBMS are the TEXT columns for the CLOB data type.

A.1   Core Commands

```
1   CREATE TABLE person (
2       sid             varchar(40)   NOT NULL,
3       published       char(5)       NOT NULL
4                       CHECK (published IN ('true','false'))
5                       DEFAULT 'false',
6       uid             varchar(60)   NOT NULL,
7       version         char(5)       NOT NULL,
8       date            varchar(60),
9       initials        char(8),
10      title           char(20),
11      firstname       varchar(50),
12      lastname        varchar(50),
13      PRIMARY KEY (uid, version),
14      UNIQUE (sid)
15  );
16
17  CREATE TABLE course (
18      sid             varchar(40)   NOT NULL,
19      published       char(5)       NOT NULL
20                      CHECK (published IN ('true','false'))
21                      DEFAULT 'false',
```

```
22    uid                  varchar(60)  NOT NULL,
23    version              char(5)      NOT NULL,
24    date                 varchar(60),
25    name                 varchar(200),
26    semester             varchar(60),
27    lectureruid          varchar(60),
28    lecturerversion      char(5),
29    PRIMARY KEY (uid, version),
30    UNIQUE (sid),
31    FOREIGN KEY (lectureruid, lecturerversion)
32            REFERENCES person(uid, version)
33    );
34
35    CREATE TABLE assignment (
36    sid                  varchar(40)  NOT NULL,
37    published            char(5)      NOT NULL
38            CHECK (published IN ('true','false'))
39            DEFAULT 'false',
40    uid                  varchar(60)  NOT NULL,
41    version              char(5)      NOT NULL,
42    date                 varchar(60),
43    authoruid            varchar(60),
44    authorversion        char(5),
45    number               varchar(120),
46    dateofissue          varchar(120),
47    deadline             varchar(120),
48    courseuid            varchar(60),
49    courseversion        char(5),
50    PRIMARY KEY (uid, version),
51    UNIQUE (sid),
52    FOREIGN KEY (courseuid, courseversion)
53            REFERENCES course(uid, version),
54    FOREIGN KEY (authoruid, authorversion)
55            REFERENCES person(uid, version)
56    );
57
58    CREATE TABLE question (
59    sid                  varchar(40)  NOT NULL,
60    published            char(5)      NOT NULL
61            CHECK (published IN ('true','false'))
```

```
62              DEFAULT 'false',
63      uid             varchar(60)    NOT NULL,
64      version         char(5)        NOT NULL,
65      date            varchar(60),
66      authoruid       varchar(60),
67      authorversion   char(5),
68      marks           varchar(60),
69      paragraph       text,
70      PRIMARY KEY (uid, version),
71      UNIQUE (sid),
72      FOREIGN KEY (authoruid, authorversion)
73              REFERENCES person(uid, version)
74      );
75
76  CREATE TABLE part (
77      sid             varchar(40)    NOT NULL,
78      published       char(5)        NOT NULL
79              CHECK (published IN ('true','false'))
80              DEFAULT 'false',
81      uid             varchar(60)    NOT NULL,
82      version         char(5)        NOT NULL,
83      date            varchar(60),
84      authoruid       varchar(60),
85      authorversion   char(5),
86      marks           varchar(60),
87      paragraph       text,
88      PRIMARY KEY (uid, version),
89      UNIQUE (sid),
90      FOREIGN KEY (authoruid, authorversion)
91              REFERENCES person(uid, version)
92      );
93
94  CREATE TABLE examination (
95      sid             varchar(40)    NOT NULL,
96      published       char(5)        NOT NULL
97              CHECK (published IN ('true','false'))
98              DEFAULT 'false',
99      uid             varchar(60)    NOT NULL,
100     version         char(5)        NOT NULL,
101     date            varchar(60),
```

```
102      authoruid        varchar(60),
103      authorversion    char(5),
104      head             varchar(200),
105      title            varchar(200),
106      student          varchar(1000),
107      valuation        varchar(1000),
108      remarks          varchar(1000),
109      pageheader       varchar(200),
110      courseuid        varchar(60),
111      courseversion    char(5),
112   PRIMARY KEY (uid, version),
113   UNIQUE (sid),
114   FOREIGN KEY (courseuid, courseversion)
115          REFERENCES course(uid, version),
116   FOREIGN KEY (authoruid, authorversion)
117          REFERENCES person(uid, version)
118   );
119
120 CREATE TABLE figure (
121      sid              varchar(40)    NOT NULL,
122      published        char(5)        NOT NULL
123               CHECK (published IN ('true','false'))
124               DEFAULT 'false',
125      uid              varchar(60)    NOT NULL,
126      version          char(5)        NOT NULL,
127      date             varchar(60),
128      authoruid        varchar(60),
129      authorversion    char(5),
130      type             varchar(60),
131      filename         varchar(120),
132      width            varchar(40),
133      height           varchar(40),
134      sourcetype       varchar(60),
135      sourcefilename   varchar(120),
136   PRIMARY KEY (uid, version),
137   UNIQUE (sid),
138   FOREIGN KEY (authoruid, authorversion)
139          REFERENCES person(uid, version)
140   );
141
```

```
142  ---------------------------
143  --  Many-to-many relations
144  ---------------------------
145  CREATE TABLE ashasques (
146      sid         varchar(40)   NOT NULL,
147      asuid       varchar(60)   NOT NULL,
148      asversion   char(5)       NOT NULL,
149      quuid       varchar(60)   NOT NULL,
150      quversion   char(5)       NOT NULL,
151      ordinal     integer,
152  PRIMARY KEY (asuid, asversion, quuid, quversion),
153  UNIQUE (sid),
154  FOREIGN KEY (asuid, asversion)
155          REFERENCES assignment(uid,version),
156  FOREIGN KEY (quuid, quversion)
157          REFERENCES question(uid,version)
158  );
159
160  CREATE TABLE examhasques (
161      sid         varchar(40)   NOT NULL,
162      emuid       varchar(60)   NOT NULL,
163      emversion   char(5)       NOT NULL,
164      quuid       varchar(60)   NOT NULL,
165      quversion   char(5)       NOT NULL,
166      ordinal     integer,
167  PRIMARY KEY (emuid, emversion, quuid, quversion),
168  UNIQUE (sid),
169  FOREIGN KEY (emuid, emversion)
170          REFERENCES examination(uid,version),
171  FOREIGN KEY (quuid, quversion)
172          REFERENCES question(uid,version)
173  );
174
175  CREATE TABLE queshaspart (
176      sid         varchar(40)   NOT NULL,
177      quuid       varchar(60)   NOT NULL,
178      quversion   char(5)       NOT NULL,
179      pauid       varchar(60)   NOT NULL,
180      paversion   char(5)       NOT NULL,
181      ordinal     int,
```

```
182    PRIMARY KEY (quuid, quversion, pauid, paversion),
183    UNIQUE (sid),
184    FOREIGN KEY (quuid, quversion)
185           REFERENCES question(uid, version),
186    FOREIGN KEY (pauid, paversion)
187           REFERENCES part(uid, version)
188    );
189
190    CREATE TABLE quesusesques (
191        sid            varchar(40)    NOT NULL,
192        quuid          varchar(60)    NOT NULL,
193        quversion      char(5)        NOT NULL,
194        useduid        varchar(60)    NOT NULL,
195        usedversion    char(5)        NOT NULL,
196    PRIMARY KEY (sid),
197    UNIQUE (sid),
198    FOREIGN KEY (quuid, quversion)
199           REFERENCES question(uid, version),
200    FOREIGN KEY (useduid, usedversion)
201           REFERENCES question(uid, version)
202    );
```

A.2   Extension Commands

```
1    ---------------------------------
2    -- Extension Node tables
3    ---------------------------------
4    CREATE TABLE link (
5        sid            varchar(40)    NOT NULL,
6        published      char(5)        NOT NULL
7                       CHECK (published IN ('true','false'))
8                       DEFAULT 'false',
9        uid            varchar(60)    NOT NULL,
10       version        char(5)        NOT NULL,
11       date           varchar(60),
12       internal       char(5)
13                      CHECK (internal IN ('true','false')),
14       href           varchar(200),
15       text           varchar(300),
```

```
16   PRIMARY KEY (sid),
17   UNIQUE (uid, version)
18   );
19
20   CREATE TABLE keyword (
21       sid        varchar(40)    NOT NULL,
22       published  char(5)        NOT NULL
23                  CHECK (published IN ('true','false'))
24                  DEFAULT 'false',
25       uid        varchar(60)    NOT NULL,
26       version    char(5)        NOT NULL,
27       name       varchar(250),
28   PRIMARY KEY (sid),
29   UNIQUE (uid, version)
30   );
31
32   --------------------------------
33   -- Extension Edge tables
34   --------------------------------
35   CREATE TABLE edgeinline (
36       sid        varchar(40)    NOT NULL,
37       ssid       varchar(40)    NOT NULL,
38       tsid       varchar(40)    NOT NULL,
39       published  char(5)        NOT NULL
40                  CHECK (published IN ('true','false'))
41                  DEFAULT 'false',
42       uid        varchar(60)    NOT NULL,
43       version    char(5)        NOT NULL,
44       ordinal    int            NOT NULL,
45       name       varchar(120)   NOT NULL,
46       value      text,
47   PRIMARY KEY (sid)
48   );
49
50   CREATE INDEX edgeinline_indx1 ON edgeinline(ssid, ordinal);
51   CREATE INDEX edgeinline_indx2 ON edgeinline(name, tsid);
52   CREATE INDEX edgeinline_indx3 ON edgeinline(value);
53
54   CREATE TABLE edge (
55       sid        varchar(40)    NOT NULL,
```

```
56      ssid        varchar(40)     NOT NULL,
57      tsid        varchar(40)     NOT NULL,
58      ordinal     int             NOT NULL,
59      name        varchar(120)    NOT NULL,
60   PRIMARY KEY (sid)
61   );
62
63   CREATE INDEX edge_indx1 ON edge(ssid, ordinal);
64   CREATE INDEX edge_indx2 ON edge(name, tsid);
65
66   CREATE TABLE edgeattribute (
67      ssid    varchar(40)     NOT NULL,
68      name    varchar(60)     NOT NULL,
69      value   varchar(120),
70   PRIMARY KEY (ssid, name)
71   );
72
73   CREATE TABLE edgecomment (
74      sid         varchar(40)     NOT NULL,
75      ssid        varchar(40)     NOT NULL,
76      ordinal     int             NOT NULL,
77      comment     varchar(3000),
78   PRIMARY KEY (sid)
79   );
80
81   CREATE INDEX edgecomment_indx1 ON edgecomment(ssid, ordinal);
82
83   CREATE TABLE edgeprocinstr (
84      sid         varchar(40)     NOT NULL,
85      ssid        varchar(40)     NOT NULL,
86      ordinal     int             NOT NULL,
87      target      varchar(30)     NOT NULL,
88      data        text,
89   PRIMARY KEY (sid)
90   );
91
92   CREATE INDEX edgepi_indx1 ON edgeprocinstr(ssid, ordinal);
```

A.3 Presentation Commands

```
 1   CREATE TABLE xsl_stylesheet (
 2       sid              varchar(40)    NOT NULL,
 3       published        char(5)        NOT NULL
 4                CHECK (Published IN ('true','false'))
 5                DEFAULT 'false',
 6       uid              varchar(60)    NOT NULL,
 7       version          char(5)        NOT NULL,
 8       date             varchar(60),
 9       authorUID        varchar(60),
10       authorVersion    char(5),
11       starttags        text,
12       endtags          varchar(100),
13       description      varchar(300),
14    PRIMARY KEY (uid, version),
15    UNIQUE (sid)
16    );
17
18   ALTER TABLE xsl_stylesheet ADD CONSTRAINT xs_FK1
19       FOREIGN KEY (authoruid, authorversion)
20       REFERENCES Person(uid, version);
21
22   CREATE TABLE xsl_template (
23       sid              varchar(40)    NOT NULL,
24       published        char(5)        NOT NULL
25                CHECK (published IN ('true','false'))
26                DEFAULT 'false',
27       uid              varchar(60)    NOT NULL,
28       version          char(5)        NOT NULL,
29       date             varchar(60),
30       authorUID        varchar(60),
31       authorVersion    char(5),
32       match            varchar(120),
33       name             varchar(60),
34       priority         varchar(60),
35       mode             varchar(60),
36       component        text,
37       description      varchar(300),
38    PRIMARY KEY (uid, version),
```

```
39    UNIQUE (sid)
40    );
41
42    ALTER TABLE xsl_template ADD CONSTRAINT xt_FK1
43        FOREIGN KEY (AuthorUID, AuthorVersion)
44        REFERENCES Person(UID, Version);
45
46    CREATE TABLE xsl_style_template (
47        sUid        varchar(60) NOT NULL,
48        sVersion    char(5)     NOT NULL,
49        tUid        varchar(60) NOT NULL,
50        tVersion    char(5)     NOT NULL,
51      PRIMARY KEY (suid, sversion, tuid, tversion)
52    );
53
54    ALTER TABLE xsl_style_template ADD CONSTRAINT xst_FK1
55        FOREIGN KEY (suid,sversion)
56        REFERENCES xsl_stylesheet(uid,version);
57    ALTER TABLE xsl_style_template ADD CONSTRAINT xst_FK2
58        FOREIGN KEY (tuid,tversion)
59        REFERENCES xsl_template(uid,version);
60
61    CREATE TABLE xsl_node_style (
62        sid         varchar(60)     NOT NULL,
63        nuid        varchar(60),
64        nversion    char(5),
65        nodename    varchar(120),
66        suid        varchar(60)     NOT NULL,
67        sversion    char(5) NOT NULL,
68      PRIMARY KEY (sid)
69    );
70
71    ALTER TABLE xsl_node_style ADD CONSTRAINT xns_FK1
72        FOREIGN KEY (suid,sversion)
73        REFERENCES xsl_stylesheet(uid,version);
74
75    CREATE TABLE xsl_node_template (
76        sid         varchar(60)     NOT NULL,
77        nuid        varchar(60),
78        nversion    char(5),
```

```
79    nodename  varchar(120),
80    tuid      varchar(60)    NOT NULL,
81    tversion  char(5)        NOT NULL,
82  PRIMARY KEY (sid)
83  );
84  ALTER TABLE xsl_node_template ADD CONSTRAINT xnt_FK1
85    FOREIGN KEY (tuid,tversion)
86    REFERENCES xsl_template(uid,version);
```

A.4 Metadata Commands

```
1  CREATE TABLE raxmetatable (
2      dbtable  varchar(40) NOT NULL,
3      type     char(10)    NOT NULL,
4      number   int         NOT NULL,
5    PRIMARY KEY (dbtable)
6  );
7
8  CREATE TABLE raxmetacolumn (
9      tablecolumn  varchar(81)  NOT NULL,
10     dbtable      varchar(40)  NOT NULL,
11     columnname   varchar(40)  NOT NULL,
12     domain       varchar(30)  NOT NULL,
13     width        int          NOT NULL,
14     pk           char(5)      NOT NULL,
15     nnull        char(5)      NOT NULL,
16     xmlattr      char(5)      NOT NULL,
17   PRIMARY KEY (tablecolumn),
18   FOREIGN KEY (dbtable) REFERENCES raxmetatable(dbtable)
19  );
20
21  create table raxmeta1toone (
22    relname          varchar(81) NOT NULL,
23    table1           varchar(40) NOT NULL,
24    table2           varchar(40) NOT NULL,
25    insert1intoone   char(5)     NOT NULL,
26    xmlname1intoone  varchar(40) NOT NULL,
27    insertoneinto1   char(5)     NOT NULL,
28    xmlnameoneinto1  varchar(40) NOT NULL,
```

```
29      PRIMARY KEY (relname),
30      FOREIGN KEY (table1) REFERENCES raxmetatable(dbtable),
31      FOREIGN KEY (table2) REFERENCES raxmetatable(dbtable)
32   );
33
34   CREATE TABLE raxmetaoneton (
35      relname             varchar(81)   NOT NULL,
36      table1              varchar(40)   NOT NULL,
37      table2              varchar(40)   NOT NULL,
38      insertoneinton      char(5)       NOT NULL,
39      xmlnameoneinton     varchar(40)   NOT NULL,
40      insertnintoone      char(5)       NOT NULL,
41      xmlnamenintoone     varchar(40)   NOT NULL,
42      PRIMARY KEY (relname),
43      FOREIGN KEY (table1) REFERENCES raxmetatable(dbtable),
44      FOREIGN KEY (table2) REFERENCES raxmetatable(dbtable)
45   );
46
47   CREATE TABLE raxmetamton (
48      relname             varchar(40)   NOT NULL,
49      table1              varchar(40)   NOT NULL,
50      table2              varchar(40)   NOT NULL,
51      insertminton        char(5)       NOT NULL,
52      xmlnameminton       varchar(40)   NOT NULL,
53      insertnintom        char(5)       NOT NULL,
54      xmlnamenintom       varchar(40)   NOT NULL,
55      PRIMARY KEY (relname),
56      FOREIGN KEY (table1) REFERENCES raxmetatable(dbtable),
57      FOREIGN KEY (table2) REFERENCES raxmetatable(dbtable)
58   );
59
60   CREATE TABLE raxmetarelcolumn (
61      relname   varchar(81)   NOT NULL,
62      column1   varchar(81)   NOT NULL,
63      column2   varchar(81)   NOT NULL,
64      side      varchar(5),
65      PRIMARY KEY (relname, column1, column2),
66      FOREIGN KEY (column1) REFERENCES raxmetacolumn(tablecolumn),
67      FOREIGN KEY (column2) REFERENCES raxmetacolumn(tablecolumn)
68   );
```

Appendix B

HTML Documents created with RelAndXML

In this appendix, we show some screenshots with the HTML output of assignments that we stored in *RelAndXML*.

- Figure B.1 shows the assignment 10 of the course "Grundzüge der Informatik 1" from the winter semester 1999/2000, lectured by Prof. Dr. Herbert Göttler.

- Figure B.2 shows the single assignment page of the course "Konzepte von Programmierspachen 1" where questions were added during the winter semester 2001/2002. The lecturer was Prof. Dr. Herbert Göttler.

- Figure B.3 shows the assignment 2 of the course "Betriebssysteme 1", lectured by PD Dr. Klaus Barthelmann in the winter semester 2001/2002.

- Figure B.4 shows the assignment 1 of the course "Objektorientierte Programmierung in Java" which was lectured by PD Dr. Klaus Barthelmann in the winter semester 2002/2003.

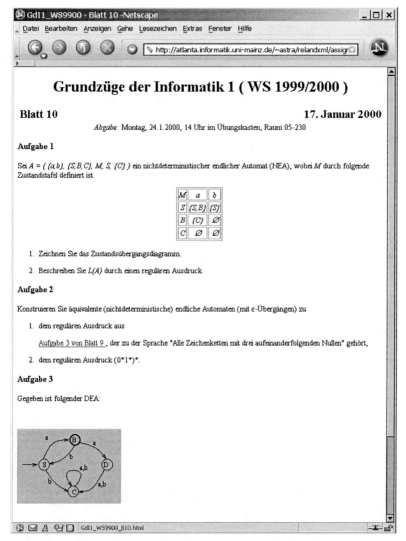

Figure B.1: Assignment 10 of the course "Grundzüge der Informatik 1"

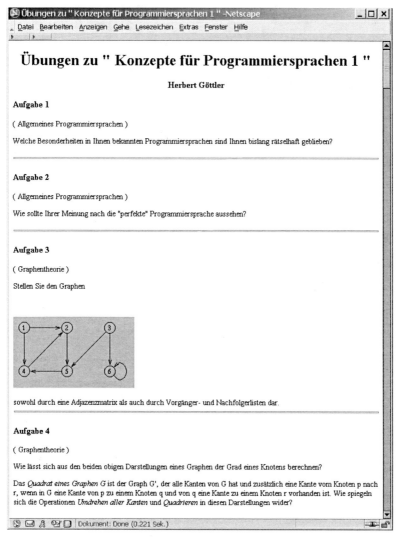

Figure B.2: Questions for the course "Konzepte von Programmiersprachen 1"

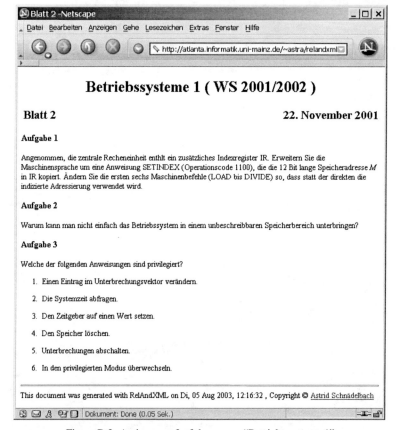

Figure B.3: Assignment 2 of the course "Betriebssysteme 1"

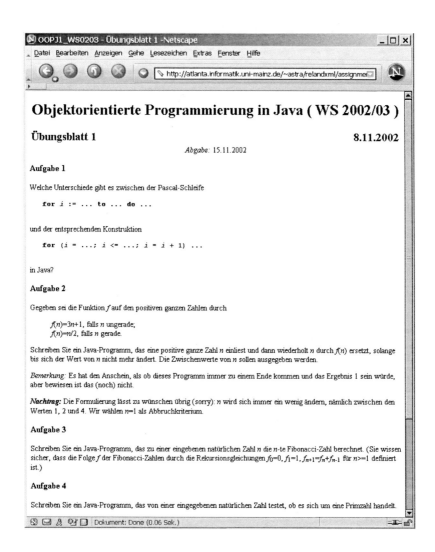

Figure B.4: Assignment 1 of the course "Objektorientierte Programmierung in Java"

References

[A⁺01]   Eric Armstrong et al. *Working with XML: The Java API for Xml Processing (JAXP) Tutorial – Part III: XML and the Document Object Model (DOM)*. `http://java.sun.com/xml/jaxp/dist/1.1/docs/tutorial/dom/index.html`, 2001. Verified on 27 June 2003.

[Ada03]   Adabas. `http://www.softwareag.com/adabas`, verified on 30 May 2003.

[ASW01]   Eric Armstrong, Tom Santos, and Steve Wilson. *Understanding the TreeModel: Why 'Less Is More' is an Elegant Design*. `http://java.sun.com/products/jfc/tsc/articles/jtree/index.html`, 2001. Verified on 26 June 2003.

[BFRS02] Philip Bohannon, Juliana Freire, Prasan Roy, and Jérôme Siméon. From XML Schema to Relations: A Cost-Based Approach to XML Storage. In *ICDE*, 2002.

[Bou01]   Ronald Bourret. Mapping DTDs to Databases. URL: `http://www.xml.com/pub/a/2001/05/09/dtdtodbs.html`, May 2001.

[Bou03a] Ronald Bourret. XML and Databases, January 2003. `http://www.rpbourret.com/xml/XMLAndDatabases.htm`.

[Bou03b] Ronald Bourret. XML Database Products, March 2003. `http://www.rpbourret.com/xml/XMLDatabaseProds.htm`.

[Bou03c] Ronald Bourret. XML-DBMS. `http://www.rpbourret.com/xmldbms/`, verified on 30 May 2003.

[CFP00]   Stefano Ceri, Piero Fraternali, and Stefano Paraboschi. XML: Current Developments and Future Challenges for the Database Community. In *EDBT 2000*, LNCS 1777, pages 3–17, 2000.

[COR03] CORBA. http://www.corba.org, verified on 30 May 2003.

[DB203] IBM DB2 Universal Database. http://www.ibm.com/software/data/db2/udb/, verified on 30 May 2003.

[DBL03] DBLP Computer Science Library. http://dblp.uni-trier.de, verified on 30 May 2003.

[DFS99] Alin Deutsch, Mary Fernandez, and Dan Suciu. Storing Semistructured Data with STORED. In *Proceedings of the ACM SIGMOD International Conference on Management of Data*, 1999. Available from http://www.research.att.com/~suciu.

[DJL00] DOM Java Language Binding. http://www.w3.org/TR/DOM-Level-2-Core/java-binding.html, 2000.

[DOM03] Document Object Model. http://www.w3.org/DOM/, verified on 30 May 2003.

[EM02a] Andrew Eisenberg and Jim Melton. An Early Look at XQuery. *ACM SIGMOD Records*, 31(4), December 2002.

[EM02b] Andrew Eisenberg and Jim Melton. SQL/XML is Making Good Progress. *ACM SIGMOD Records*, 31(2), June 2002.

[EN00] Ramez Elmasri and Shamkant B. Navathe. *Fundamentals of Database Systems*. Addison-Wesley, Reading, Massachusetts, 3rd edition, 2000.

[eXc03] eXcelon Corporation. http://www.exln.com, verified on 30 May 2003.

[FK99a] Daniela Florescu and Donald Kossmann. A Performance Evaluation of Alternative Mapping Schemes for Storing XML Data in a Relational Database. Technical Report 3680, INRIA, Rocquencourt, May 1999.

[FK99b] Daniela Florescu and Donald Kossmann. Storing and querying XML data using an RDBMS. *IEEE Data Engineering Bulletin*, 22(3):27–34, 1999.

[Fla00] David Flanagan. *Java Examples in a Nutshell*. O'Reilly, 2000.

[Gra02] Mark Graves. *Designing XML Databases*. Prentice Hall PTR, 2002.

[HC02] Cay Horstmann and Gary Cornell. *Core Java 2*, volume II - Advanced Features. Sun Microsystems Press (Prentice Hall), 5th edition, 2002.

[HC03]   Cay Horstmann and Gary Cornell. *Core Java 2*, volume I - Fundamentals. Sun Microsystems Press (Prentice Hall), 6th edition, 2003.

[Heu02]   Andreas Heuer. Objektorientierte Datenbanken – Rückblick oder Ausblick? – Das Los des Joschka Fischer. *GI-Fachgruppentreffen Datenbanken*, October 2002. Conference manuskript, available from http://www.datenbank-portal.de/Programm.27.0.html.

[HM02]   Elliote Rusty Harold and W. Scott Means. *XML in a Nutshell*. O'Reilly, second edition, 2002.

[HTM99]   HTML 4.01 Specification. http://www.w3.org/TR/html401, 1999.

[Inf03a]   Infonyte. http://www.infonyte.com, verified on 30 May 2003.

[Inf03b]   IBM Informix. http://www.ibm.com/software/data/informix/, verified on 30 May 2003.

[Jav03]   Java 2 Platform, Standard Edition, v 1.4.1 API Specification. http://java.sun.com/j2se/1.4.1/docs/api/, verified on 25 July 2003.

[JDB03]   JDBC API Documentation. http://java.sun.com/j2se/1.4.2/docs/guide/jdbc/index.html, verified on 30 June 2003.

[Kay01]   Michael Kay. *XSLT 2nd Edition: Programmer's Reference*. Wrox Press, 2001.

[KC02]   Thomas Kudrass and Matthias Conrad. Management of XML Documents in Object-Relational Databases. In *XML-Based Data Management and Multimedia Egineering – EDBT 2002 Workshops*, pages 210–227, 2002.

[KKR01]   Gerti Kappel, Elisabeth Kapsammer, and Werner Retschitzegger. Architectural Issues for Integrating XML and Relational Database Systems - The X-Ray Approach. In *Workshop XML Technologies and Software Engineering (XSE 2001)*, Toronto, Canada, May 2001.

[KM00]   Meike Klettke and Holger Meyer. XML and object-relational database systems - enhancing structural mappings based on statistics. In *Proc. WebDB 2000*, May 2000.

[KM03]   Meike Klettke and Holger Meyer. *XML & Datenbanken – Konzepte, Sprachen und Systeme*. dpunkt, Heidelberg, 2003.

[Kud01]   Thomas Kudrass. Management of XML Documents without Schema in Re-
            lational Database Systems. In *Proc. of the OOPSLA Workshop on Objects,
            <XML> and Databases*, October 2001.

[Mel03]   Jim Melton. *Advanced SQL:1999 – Understanding Object-Relational and
            Other Advanced Features*. Morgan Kaufmann Publishers, 2003.

[MKF+03]   Jan-Eike Michels, Krishna Kulkarni, Christopher M. Farrar, Andrew Eisen-
            berg, Nelson Mattos, and Hugh Darwen. The SQL Standard. *it – Information
            Technology*, 45(1):30–38, February 2003.

[MS02]   Jim Melton and Alan R. Simon. *SQL:1999 – Understanding Relational Lan-
            guage Components*. Morgan Kaufmann Publishers, 2002.

[MSS03]   Microsoft SQL Server. http://www.microsoft.com/sql, verified
            on 30 May 2003.

[ODM03]   Object Database Management Group. http://www.odmg.org, verified
            on 24 July 2003.

[Ora03]   Oracle. http://www.oracle.com, verified on 30 May 2003.

[POE03]   POET Software Corporation. http://www.poet.com, verified on 30
            May 2003.

[Pos03]   PostgreSQL. http://www.postgresql.org, verified on 2 June 2003.

[REL03]   RELAX   NG.   http://www.oasis-open.org/committees/
            relax-ng/, verified on 30 May 2003.

[RP02]   Kanda Runapongsa and Jignesh M. Patel. Storing and Querying XML Data
            in Object-Relational DBMSs. In *EDBT 2002 - Workshop XMLDM*, March
            2002.

[SAX03]   Simple API for XML. http://www.saxproject.org, verified on 30
            May 2003.

[Sch03a]   Schematron.   http://www.ascc.net/xml/resource/
            schematron/, verified on 30 May 2003.

[Sch03b]   Harald Schöning. *XML und Datenbanken – Konzepte und Systeme*. Hanser,
            München, 2003.

[SGM86]   Standard Generalized Markup Language (SGML). ISO 8879, 1986.

[SQL03] SQLX Group. http://www.sqlx.org, verified on 24 July 2003.

[SSB⁺01] Jayavel Shanmugasundaram, Eugene J. Shekita, Rimon Barr, Michael J. Carey, Bruce G. Lindsay, Hamid Pirahesh, and Berthold Reinwald. Efficiently publishing relational data as XML documents. *VLDB Journal*, 10:133–154, 2001.

[STH⁺99] Jayavel Shanmugasundaram, Kristin Tufte, Gang He, Chun Zhang, David J. DeWitt, and Jeffrey F. Naughton. Relational Databases for Querying XML Documents: Limitations and Opportunities. In *Proceedings of the 25th VLDB Conference, Edinburgh, Scotland*, pages 302–314, 1999.

[SYU99] Takeyuki Shimura, Masatoshi Yoshikawa, and Shunsuke Uemura. Storage and Retrieval of XML Documents Using Object-Relational Databases. In *Proceedings of the DEXA'99*, pages 206–217, 1999.

[Tam03] Tamino XML Server. http://www.softwareag.com/tamino/, verified on 30 May 2003.

[Tid01] Doug Tidwell. *XSLT: Mastering XML Transformations*. O'Reilly, 2001.

[Tür03] Can Türker. *SQL:1999 & SQL:2003*. dpunkt, Heidelberg, 2003.

[TVB⁺02] Igor Tatarinov, Stratis D. Viglas, Kevin Beyer, Jayavel Shanmugasundaram, Eugene Shekita, and Chun Zhang. Storing and Querying Ordered XML Using a Relational Database System. *ACM SIGMOD*, 2002.

[Uni03] Unicode. http://www.unicode.org, verified on 30 May 2003.

[W3C03] World Wide Web Consortium (W3C). http://www.w3.org, verified on 30 May 2003.

[Wid99] Jennifer Widom. Data Management for XML – Research Directions. *IEEE Data Engineering Bulletin, Special Issue on XML*, 22(3):44–52, September 1999.

[Xal03] Xalan (XSL Processor). http://xml.apache.org/xalan-j/, verified on 30 May 2003.

[XDB03] XML:DB Initiative for XML Databases. http://www.xmldb.org, verified on 30 May 2003.

[XEd03] XML.com: Editors. http://www.xml.com/pub/pt/3, verified on 28 July 2003.

[Xer03]   Xerces (XML Parser). `http://xml.apache.org/xerces2-j/`, ver-
            ified on 30 May 2003.

[XHT02]   XHTML 1.0: The Extensible HyperText Markup Language (Second Edition).
            `http://www.w3.org/TR/xhtml1`, 2002.

[XIn01]   XML Information Set: W3C Recommendation. `http://www.w3.org/`
            `TR/xml-infoset/`, October 2001.

[Xin03]   Xindice. `http://xml.apache.org/xindice`, verified on 30 May
            2003.

[XML00]   eXtensible Markup Language (XML) 1.0 (Second Edition): W3C Recom-
            mendation. `http://www.w3.org/TR/2000/REC-xml-20001006`,
            October 2000.

[XML02]   Extensible Markup Language (XML) 1.1: W3C Candidate Recommendation
            15 October 2002. `http://www.w3.org/TR/xml11`, 2002. Verified on
            4 June 2003.

[XMQ03]   XML Query. http://www.w3.org/XML/Query, verified on 23 June 2003.

[XMS01a]   XML   Schema   Part   0:   Primer.   `http://www.w3.org/TR/`
            `xmlschema-0`, 2001.

[XMS01b]   XML   Schema   Part   1:   Structures.   `http://www.w3.org/TR/`
            `xmlschema-1`, 2001.

[XMS01c]   XML   Schema   Part   2:   Datatypes.   `http://www.w3.org/TR/`
            `xmlschema-2`, 2001.

[XPa99]   XML Path Language (XPath), Version 1.0: W3C Recommendation. `http:`
            `//www.w3.org/TR/1999/REC-xpath-19991116`, November 1999.

[XQL98]   XML-QL: A Query Language for XML Submission to the World
            Wide Web Consortium 19-August-1998.   `http://www.w3.org/TR/`
            `NOTE-xml-ql`, 1998. Verified on 23 June 2003.

[XQu03]   XQuery 1.0: An XML Query Language, W3C Working Draft 02 May 2003.
            http://www.w3.org/TR/xquery/, verified on 4 June 2003.

[XSL99]   XSL Transformations Version 1.0: W3C Recommendation. `http://www.`
            `w3.org/TR/xslt`, November 1999.

[XSL03]   The Extensible Stylesheet Language Family (XSL). `http://www.w3.`
          `org/Style/XSL/`, verified on July 28 2003.

[YASU01] Masatoshi Yoshikawa, Toshiyuki Amagasa, Takeyuki Shimura, and Shunsuke
          Uemura. XRel: a path-based approach to storage and retrieval of XML docu-
          ments using relational databases. *ACM Transactions on Internet Technology
          (TOIT)*, 1(1):110–141, 2001.

List of Abbreviations

ANSI	American National Standards Institute
API	Application Programming Interface
CSS	Cascading StyleSheet
DBMS	Database Management System
DDL	Data Definition Language
DML	Data Manipulation Language
DOM	Document Object Model
DTD	Document Type Definition
EER model	Extended Entity-Relationship model
HTML	Hypertext Markup Language
HXD	Hybrid XML Database
IDL	Interface Definition Language
ISO	International Organization Standardization
NXD	Native XML Database
ODBC	Open Database Connectivity
ODMG	Object Database Management Group
ORDBMS	Object-Relational Database Management System
RDBMS	Relational Database Management System
SAX	Simple API for XML
sid	system identifier
SGML	Standard Generalized Markup Language
SQL	Structured Query Language
SQL/PSM	Persistent Stored Modules (Part of the SQL standard)
SQL/XML	XML-Related Specifications (Part of the SQL standard)

uid	user identifier
URI	Uniform Resource Identifier
URL	Uniform Resource Locator
URN	Uniform Resource Name
W3C	World Wide Web Consortium
XEDB	XML Enabled Database
XML	eXtensible Markup Language
XML:DB	Initiative for XML Databases
XPath	XML Path Language
XQuery	XML Query Language
XSL-FO	XSL Formatting Objects
XSL	eXtensible Stylesheet Language
XSLT	eXtensible Stylesheet Language for Transformations

List of Figures

List of Listings

List of Tables

Index

Lebenslauf

Astrid Susanne Schnädelbach, geboren am 26. Juli 1972 in Kaiserslautern

Hochschulbildung

12-2000 – 02-2004	Promotion in Informatik an der Johannes Gutenberg-Universität Mainz
10-1995 – 02-1999	Studium der Mathematik mit Nebenfach Informatik an der Johannes Gutenberg-Universität Mainz Abschluß: Diplom-Mathematikerin
09-1994 – 05-1995	Austauschstudentin an der University of Waterloo, Kanada
10-1991 – 08-1994	Studium der Mathematik mit Nebenfach Informatik an der Universität Mannheim

Berufstätigkeit

03-1999 – 02-2003	wissenschaftliche Mitarbeiterin am Institut für Informatik am Fachbereich Mathematik und Informatik der Johannes Gutenberg-Universität Mainz
09-2002 – 02-2003 und 03-2001 – 08-2001	Dozentin bei der IBM IT-Akademie in Mainz
07-1997 – 09-1999	freie Mitarbeiterin auf Teilzeitbasis bei der Subito Software AG, Mörfelden-Walldorf
04-1997 – 07-1997	wissenschaftliche Hilfskraft am Fachbereich Mathematik der Johannes Gutenberg-Universität Mainz
10-1993 - 02-1994	wissenschaftliche Hilfskraft an der Fakultät für Mathematik und Informatik, Universität Mannheim

Schulbildung

1982 – 1991	Kurfürst-Ruprecht-Gymnasium, Neustadt / Weinstraße Abschluß: Allgemeine Hochschulreife
1978 – 1982	August-Becker-Schule, Lachen-Speyerdorf

Mainz, im Februar 2004